OSAMA BIN LADEN

OSAMA
BIN LADEN

Other titles in the
People Who Made History series:

PEOPLE
WHO MADE
HISTORY

OSAMA
BIN LADEN

Wim Coleman and Pat Perrin, *Book Editors*

Bruce Glassman, *Vice President*
Bonnie Szumski, *Publisher*
Helen Cothran, *Managing Editor*

GREENHAVEN PRESS
An imprint of Thomson Gale, a part of The Thomson Corporation

THOMSON
GALE

Detroit • New York • San Francisco • San Diego • New Haven, Conn.
Waterville, Maine • London • Munich

© 2006 Thomson Gale, a part of The Thomson Corporation.

Thomson and Star Logo are trademarks and Gale and Greenhaven Press are registered trademarks used herein under license.

For more information, contact
Greenhaven Press
27500 Drake Rd.
Farmington Hills, MI 48331-3535
Or you can visit our Internet site at http://www.gale.com

LIBRARY OF CONGRESS CATALOGING-IN-PUBLICATION DATA

Osama bin Laden / Wim Coleman and Pat Perrin, book editors.
  p. cm. — (People who made history)
Includes bibliographical references and index.
ISBN 0-7377-2593-1 (lib. : alk. paper)
  1. bin Laden, Osama, 1957– . 2. Terrorists—Saudi Arabia—Biography.
3. Terrorism—Religious aspects—Islam. I. Coleman, Wim. II. Perrin, Pat. III. Series.
HV6430.B55O824 2006
958.104'6'092—dc22   2005046320
[B]

Printed in the United States of America

CONTENTS

Chapter 3: Bin Laden's War Against America

FOREWORD

In the vast and colorful pageant of human history, a handful of individuals stand out. They are the men and women who have come variously to be called "great," "leading," "brilliant," "pivotal," or "infamous" because they and their deeds forever changed their own society or the world as a whole. Some were political or military leaders—kings, queens, presidents, generals, and the like—whose policies, conquests, or innovations reshaped the maps and futures of countries and entire continents. Among those falling into this category were the formidable Roman statesman/general Julius Caesar, who extended Rome's power into Gaul (what is now France); Caesar's lover and ally, the notorious Egyptian queen Cleopatra, who challenged the strongest male rulers of her day; and England's stalwart Queen Elizabeth I, whose defeat of the mighty Spanish Armada saved England from subjugation.

Some of history's other movers and shakers were scientists or other thinkers whose ideas and discoveries altered the way people conduct their everyday lives or view themselves and their place in nature. The electric light and other remarkable inventions of Thomas Edison, for example, revolutionized almost every aspect of home-life and the workplace; and the theories of naturalist Charles Darwin lit the way for biologists and other scientists in their ongoing efforts to understand the origins of living things, including human beings.

Still other people who made history were religious leaders and social reformers. The struggles of the Arabic prophet Muhammad more than a thousand years ago led to the establishment of one of the world's great religions—Islam; and the efforts and personal sacrifices of an American reverend named Martin Luther King Jr. brought about major improvements in race relations and the justice system in the United States.

Each anthology in the People Who Made History series begins with an introductory essay that provides a general overview of the individual's life, times, and contributions. The group of essays that follow are chosen for their accessibility to a young adult audience and carefully edited in consideration of the reading and comprehension levels of that audience. Some of the essays are by noted historians, professors, and other experts. Others are excerpts from contemporary writings by or about the pivotal individual in question. To aid the reader in choosing the material of immediate interest or need, an annotated table of contents summarizes the article's main themes and insights.

Each volume also contains extensive research tools, including a collection of excerpts from primary source documents pertaining to the individual under discussion. The volumes are rounded out with an extensive bibliography and a comprehensive index.

Plutarch, the renowned first-century Greek biographer and moralist, crystallized the idea behind Greenhaven's People Who Made History when he said, "To be ignorant of the lives of the most celebrated men of past ages is to continue in a state of childhood all our days." Indeed, since it is people who make history, every modern nation, organization, institution, invention, artifact, and idea is the result of the diligent efforts of one or more individuals, living or dead; and it is therefore impossible to understand how the world we live in came to be without examining the contributions of these individuals.

INTRODUCTION: OSAMA BIN LADEN IN CONTEXT

It seems likely that September 11, 2001, has become as renowned a date in American history as July 4, 1776—albeit for reasons that Americans wish they could forget. September 11 was the day when Islamist terrorists hijacked and deliberately crashed two commercial airliners into New York's World Trade Center, and another into the Pentagon near Washington, D.C. A fourth airliner, apparently targeting the U.S. Capitol, the White House, or the presidential retreat at Camp David, crashed near Shanksville, Pennsylvania, after passengers rebelled against the hijackers. The Twin Towers of the Trade Center were destroyed completely, and the Pentagon was badly damaged; overall, nearly three thousand people were killed. Scarcely had the attacks occurred before a suspect was named. "There are good indications that persons linked to Osama bin Laden may be responsible for these attacks,"[1] a U.S. intelligence official said on September 12.

It was not the first time Americans had heard of Osama bin Laden. On August 20, 1998, President Bill Clinton had described him as "perhaps the preeminent organizer and financier of international terrorism in the world today."[2] But it was only after Bin Laden brought terrorism to American shores on September 11, 2001, that his name became universally known. Ever since that infamous day, Americans have found themselves under threat not from a nation led by a head of state, but from a sprawling guerrilla organization led by a shadowy individual. And since that day, Americans have urgently needed to know who this man is, what he is capable of, and what lies behind his implacable hatred of the West.

BEGINNINGS OF A HOLY WARRIOR

Bin Laden was born on March 10 or July 30, 1957, in Riyadh, Saudi Arabia, one of construction magnate Muhammad bin Laden's more than fifty children by a number of different

12

wives, and the last of his sons. An immigrant from Yemen, the elder Bin Laden was a self-made billionaire, a close friend of Saudi Arabia's royal family, and one of the Middle East's most powerful and influential men. He was also a devout Muslim who took pride in restoring and renovating Islamic holy sites. Osama (the name means "young lion" in Arabic) learned his lifelong piety from his father, and he was undoubtedly deeply affected when Muhammad died in a helicopter crash in 1968.

For at least a decade after his father's death, Osama seemed destined for a prominent role in the family construction business. In 1979 he graduated from King Abdul Aziz University in Jeddah, Saudi Arabia, with a degree in civil engineering. But that same year, the Soviet Union invaded Afghanistan, and Bin Laden's life took a drastic turn. Like many young Muslim men worldwide, he felt drawn to the Afghan jihad (a word that, though commonly interpreted as "holy war," more accurately translates as "effort" or "struggle"). In the years that followed, Bin Laden repeatedly went to Pakistan and Afghanistan to assist the Afghan mujahideen (Muslim holy warriors) against the Soviets. Ironically, he was then an ally of the United States, since the CIA supported the Afghan fighters with billions of dollars in aid.

At first Bin Laden's participation in the Afghan war consisted primarily of providing money, facilitating construction projects, and conducting international recruitment. But as the war continued, Bin Laden threw himself personally into the struggle, experiencing deadly combat in the 1987 battle of Jaji. By the time the Soviets retreated from Afghanistan two years later, he had been wounded at least twice.

Bin Laden's global outlook was profoundly shaped by the Soviet-Afghan War. Ever since the Soviet defeat, he has held an exaggerated estimate of the role played in the conflict by the so-called Afghan Arabs (Muslim fighters who had come to Afghanistan from other countries). Because the Soviet Union came to an end soon after the Soviet-Afghan War, Bin Laden came to believe that the Afghan-Arab mujahideen literally brought about the fall of a superpower. Bin Laden began to dream of duplicating this success elsewhere and set about creating a guerrilla organization while still in Afghanistan. Eventually dubbed al Qaeda (Arabic for "the base") by the U.S. government, the organization consisted at first of Afghan Arabs and was intended to spread jihad against all perceived enemies of Islam. After the Soviet defeat in 1989, Bin Laden returned to Saudi Arabia, where he continued to build al Qaeda and was celebrated as an international Islamist hero.

AN ENEMY OF THE SAUDIS AND THE WEST

Discontentment soon set in. After the heroic struggle in Afghanistan, Bin Laden found it hard to return to the more mundane affairs of his family's business. Moreover, his long-standing dismay with the Saudi royal family's corruption and its cozy relationship with the West grew deeper. The breaking point came in 1990, when Iraq, under the leadership of the brutal dictator Saddam Hussein, invaded the small Arabic nation of Kuwait. Saudi Arabia, a neighbor to both Iraq and Kuwait, seemed under imminent threat from Hussein's aggression. Bin Laden offered to raise an army of Islamist warriors to defend Saudi Arabia and drive Hussein out of Kuwait. Having participated in the defeat of Soviet forces in Afghanistan, Bin Laden was confident that he and his followers would make short work of a petty upstart like Hussein.

The Saudi regime, however, coolly rejected Bin Laden's offer, turning instead to the United States for help. In Bin Laden's mind, accepting the aid of Western infidels to defend the sacred Arabian peninsula was a great betrayal of Islam; the establishment of U.S. military bases in Saudi Arabia struck him as the ultimate humiliation, rendering the region nothing more than an American colony. Soon after the United States defeated Hussein in the Persian Gulf War of 1991, Bin Laden went into exile from Saudi Arabia and became as unswerving a foe of his home country's regime as he was of the United States and Israel. After a brief return to Afghanistan, Bin Laden settled in the Islamist-ruled African nation of Sudan in 1992.

While Bin Laden openly pursued numerous business interests in Sudan, he covertly continued to build al Qaeda and began to instigate or influence guerrilla acts worldwide. Al Qaeda was connected with the New York World Trade Center attack of 1993, in which a truck bomb damaged Tower One and killed six people. In 1994 and 1995, the organization was behind failed assassination plots against U.S. president Bill Clinton and Pope John Paul II when each made separate visits to the Philippines. Bin Laden also had a hand in the successful 1995 attack on the Saudi-Arabian National

Guard Building in Riyadh, an event that killed five Americans and two others. During al Qaeda's early years, Bin Laden praised worldwide terrorist attacks against the West while taking care to deny responsibility for them. It is therefore difficult to determine how many such attacks are directly, or even indirectly, attributable to him.

After Saudi Arabia stripped Bin Laden of his citizenship in 1994, Sudan came under increasing pressure to turn Bin Laden over to international authorities. Some experts believe that Bin Laden was expelled by the Sudanese government; others believe that he voluntarily left Sudan to spare trouble for the country's Islamic rulers, whom he sincerely respected. In either case, Bin Laden returned to Afghanistan in May 1996. There he used old Afghan connections to help the fundamentalist Taliban regime come to power. Once in power, the Taliban returned the favor by refusing to turn Bin Laden over to the international community for his alleged connection to terrorist acts and his increasingly outspoken threats against the West.

ESCALATING ATTACKS

In Afghanistan Bin Laden quickly mobilized his al Qaeda network. On June 25, 1996, a month or so after Bin Laden fled Sudan, a truck bomb exploded outside the Khobar military complex in Dhahran, Saudi Arabia, killing nineteen U.S. soldiers and one Saudi, and wounding 372 others. Although the Khobar Towers bombing was initially blamed solely on the Lebanese militant organization Hizballah, *The 9/11 Commission Report* of 2004 suggests that Bin Laden helped facilitate the attack.

More attacks followed. Bin Laden was clearly connected with two nearly simultaneous bombings of U.S. embassies in Tanzania and Kenya on August 7, 1998; 225 people were killed and more than 4,000 injured in these attacks. After the bombings, Clinton ordered missile strikes at Sudan and Afghanistan in a failed attempt to kill Bin Laden and cripple al Qaeda's training facilities. Undaunted, al Qaeda struck again. On October 12, 2000, suicide bombers badly damaged the destroyer USS *Cole* as it refueled in the port of Aden, Yemen. Seventeen U.S. sailors were killed, and 39 others were injured. An FBI investigation showed that al Qaeda carried out the attack and that Bin Laden himself planned it. Less than a year later al Qaeda carried out the attacks of September 11, 2001, and with them came America's burning need to understand Bin Laden.

The bare-bones facts of Bin Laden's life before September 11, 2001, show that he and al Qaeda did not simply appear out of nowhere on that terrible day; he already had a long, if generally neglected, history of hostility toward the West. But the facts fail to satisfy at a deeper level. They do not explain Bin Laden's motivations and mindset—much less do they predict what he might do in the future.

THE PSYCHOLOGY OF AN "EVIL GENIUS"

The word *evil* has often been used as a catchall explanation of Bin Laden and his followers. In an interview with Larry King a few days after the 9/11 attacks, CBS journalist Dan Rather remarked of militants who hated and attacked America, "There are just evil people in some places."[5] This sentiment is often echoed by President George W. Bush when he refers to U.S. opponents in the war on terror as "evildoers." But some experts believe that trying to understand Bin Laden and his ilk in terms of pure evil is too simplistic.

In the wake of 9/11 the 2002 annual meeting of the World Economic Forum was themed "The Diabolical Mind." As the meeting's panel of psychologists delved into the nature of evil, Bin Laden was never far from the discussion. Alison Gopnik, professor of psychology at the University of California at Berkeley, acknowledged that there is a certain type of person, termed a psychopath, who lacks feeling and compassion and is indifferent to the sufferings of others. But Gopnik put her finger on a paradox: In order to coordinate vicious deeds on the complex, sophisticated scale of 9/11, a person must possess a sufficient degree of conscience and morality to connect with other people and motivate them to act. So however wicked his intentions, Bin Laden cannot be explained away by simple words like *evil* or *psychopathic*; to Gopnik, Bin Laden is brilliant and complex as well as extremely dangerous. To understand what drives him, some experts turn to psychology, examining his early life for keys to his personality and behavior.

For example, it is commonly believed that Bin Laden's mother, Hamida, was held in lower esteem than his father's other wives—partly because she was Syrian and therefore a foreigner, and partly because she held modern views and preferred Chanel pantsuits to the all-covering Islamic burka.

While visiting Oxford as a teenager in 1971, Bin Laden himself reportedly spoke of his mother's lowly status. As the only son of his father's so-called "slave wife," Bin Laden is said to have felt himself an outsider in his own family; as the son of a Yemeni immigrant, he is said to have felt himself an outsider in his own country. A friend of the Bin Laden family once remarked, "In a country that is obsessed with parentage, with who your great-grandfather was, Osama was almost a double outsider."[4]

It is also commonly believed Osama's early life was further complicated by his own lapses from his culture's strict Islamic faith. Concerning bin Laden's youth, terrorism expert Yossef Bodansky writes,

> Osama bin Laden started the 1970s as did many other sons of the affluent and well-connected—breaking the strict Muslim lifestyle in Saudi Arabia with sojourns in cosmopolitan Beirut. While in high school and college Osama visited Beirut often, frequenting flashy nightclubs, casinos, and bars. He was a drinker and womanizer, which often got him into bar brawls.[5]

A Sense of Belonging and a Means of Atonement

Some analysts find such information about Bin Laden's past to be revealing. It has been suggested that Bin Laden's involvement in international terror has brought him a sense of belonging that he lacked during his youth. In an article about Bin Laden and al Qaeda, Middle East expert Benjamin Orbach writes the following:

> Political psychologist Dr. Jerrold Post argues that people are drawn to political violence not purely from ideological considerations but also through personal and psychological factors, as an end in itself: "Individuals become terrorists in order to join terrorist groups and commit acts of terrorism" This view also applies to bin Ladin and his colleagues. Fighting provides them with an identity, a group that functions as a community, a respected leadership position, and a set of ideas providing a purpose to life.[6]

This assessment suggests that Bin Laden regards his own youthful backslidings as confirmation of the West's corrupting influence upon the Islamic world. Thus his leadership of al Qaeda may serve as a sort of atonement for having succumbed to Western temptations, as well as a means of turning his back upon perceived failures of his own family and culture. As Orbach also writes,

> The availability of opportunities that are simultaneously highly

attractive and forbidden by their [Islamist militants'] cultural background or identity could create a rejection of Western values along with a questioning of familiar values at home. After indulgence in what Iranian militants have called West-oxification, individuals can engage in self-loathing and a determination to punish the system, which lured them off the proper path.[7]

This psychological interpretation offers an image of a man haunted by his early life, including his own transgressions, and who is now acting out his deep-rooted hostilities on the global stage.

Unfortunately, the information underlying such an interpretation may not be fully dependable. CIA veteran Michael Scheuer, the formerly anonymous author of *Through Our Enemies' Eye: Osama bin Laden, Radical Islam, and the Future of America*, doubts that Bin Laden's mother was a family pariah—and consequently doubts that he felt himself an outsider in his own family. Scheuer cites accounts suggesting that Hamida may have been, at least for a time, Muhammad bin Laden's favorite wife. The fact that Muhammad divorced Osama's mother does not contradict this possibility. An acquaintance of the elder Bin Laden remarked that he "changed wives like you or I change cars"[8] a common practice among wealthy Saudis.

Moreover, Bin Laden himself seems to maintain an affectionate—if geographically distant—relationship with his mother even today, which suggests that he does not regard her as a corrupting modern influence. In fact, she continues to play an active role in his life. For example, while Bin Laden was in Sudan, she served as a Saudi envoy on an unsuccessful mission to bring him home. Also, when she made a public statement shortly after 9/11, her interviewer described her as "a devout Muslim never seen in public without the head-to-toe covering of a hijab [burka],"[9] suggesting that perhaps even her modernity has been overstated.

In his book *Holy War, Inc.: Inside the Secret World of Osama bin Laden*, journalist Peter L. Bergen questions other pieces of conventional wisdom about Bin Laden—for example, the claim of Bodansky and others that he was a brawler, drinker, and womanizer during his youth. Writes Bergen, "Those who know bin Laden . . . describe a deeply religious teenager who married at the age of seventeen. Perhaps Bodansky confused Osama with one of his twenty or so half-brothers."[10] Indeed, in a 2002 interview, a half-brother of Bin Laden described young

Osama as "perfect" in his religion; according to this relative, Osama considered it his duty to wake up his brothers and sisters for sunrise prayers. Such accounts do not square well with the accepted image of a drunken young Bin Laden fighting over a young woman in a bar.

So psychological explanations of Bin Laden's mindset and behavior are not necessarily supported by reliable facts. Some experts—especially Michael Scheuer—suggest a dramatically simpler approach to understanding Bin Laden: paying attention to his own words.

BIN LADEN ACCORDING TO BIN LADEN

Two days after the 9/11 attacks, *Slate* magazine writer David Plotz commented that most terrorist groups at least have comprehensible goals and "seek to participate in our world":

> But Bin Laden and his followers are alarming because they don't want anything from us. They don't want our sympathy. They want no material thing we can offer them. They don't want to participate in the community of nations. (They don't really believe in the nation-state.) They are motivated by religion, not politics. They answer to no one but their god, so they certainly won't answer to us.[11]

Plotz's contention that Bin Laden is simply a vengeful religious fanatic with no meaningful agenda has been echoed in many quarters. For example, in an address to a joint session of Congress and the American people on September 20, 2001, Bush maintained that Bin Laden and his followers are motivated by unadulterated hatred: "They hate our freedoms— our freedom of religion, our freedom of speech, our freedom to vote and assemble and disagree with each other."[12]

In a 2004 videotaped speech, Bin Laden denied Bush's claim that he and al Qaeda hated freedom. "If so," Bin Laden remarked, "then let him explain to us why we don't strike for example—Sweden?"[13] Bin Laden's retort hides the fact that his agenda discards democracy altogether. The restored caliphate he dreams of—a fundamentalist government in which a single Islamic potentate called a caliph would rule the entire Islamic world—would have no use at all for the liberties Bush spoke of. It is nonetheless true that Bin Laden's war against the West has almost nothing to do with such freedoms; he has made that abundantly clear on many occasions. The al Qaeda leader has often clearly, succinctly, and publicly stated the true motives and goals of his jihad.

THE MOTIVES OF BIN LADEN'S JIHAD

To date Bin Laden has issued two fatwas (religious decrees) declaring jihad upon the Saudi regime, Israel, and the United States. The first was issued in 1996, the second in 1998. The first (by far the longer) carries somewhat less authority in the Islamic world because it was signed solely by Bin Laden and not by Islamic leaders; nevertheless, it is a clear statement of his grievances and his mission. It places special emphasis on the need to liberate the "two Holy Places" of Islam—Mecca and Medina in Saudi Arabia—from U.S. occupation:

> The people of Islam awakened and realised that they are the main target for the aggression of the Zionist-Crusaders [Israeli-Christian] alliance. . . . The latest and the greatest of these aggressions, incurred by the Muslims since the death of the Prophet (Allah's blessing and salutations on him) is the occupation of the land of the two Holy Places—the foundation of the house of Islam, the place of the revelation, the source of the message and the place of the noble Ka'ba [the mosque in Mecca], the Qiblah [direction faced in prayer] of all Muslims— by the armies of the American Crusaders and their allies.[14]

Once again, this is no small matter for Bin Laden. When the United States established military bases in Saudi Arabia after Hussein's invasion of Kuwait, Bin Laden felt that both

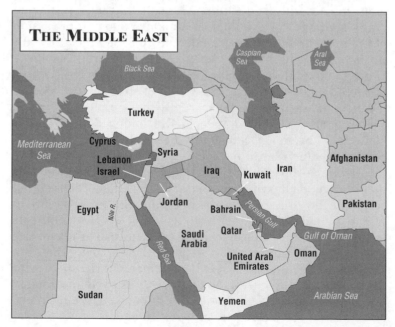

THE MIDDLE EAST

Saudis and Americans had defied the deathbed command of Islam's founder, the prophet Muhammad: "Let there be no two religions in Arabia." Some analysts have noted that, when France and England carved up the Arabic world into nation-states after World War I and colonized the region for a time, they took care to respect Islamic feelings and avoided creating a strong military presence in the Arabian peninsula. Thus the establishment of U.S. military bases in Saudi Arabia struck Bin Laden as a profound and unprecedented sacrilege.

The second, shorter fatwa of 1998 has been more influential, largely because it was cosigned by several prominent militant leaders, including Ayman al-Zawahiri, head of the Egyptian Islamic Jihad (EIJ). It lists specific grievances against the West, including the U.S. occupation of the Islamic holy land, the devastation inflicted by Americans upon the people of Iraq, U.S. complicity in the Israeli occupation of Jerusalem, and atrocities committed by Israelis against Muslims. It is in this fatwa that Bin Laden makes an especially infamous pronouncement, setting the stage for the attacks of 9/11:

> The ruling to kill the Americans and their allies—civilians and military—is an individual duty for every Muslim who can do it in any country in which it is possible to do it, in order to liberate the al-Aqsa Mosque [Jerusalem] and the holy mosque [Mecca] from their grip, and in order for their armies to move out of all the lands of Islam, defeated and unable to threaten any Muslim. This is in accordance with the words of Almighty God, "and fight the pagans all together as they fight you all together," and "fight them until there is no more tumult or oppression, and there prevail justice and faith in God."[15]

Both Westerners and the majority of the world's Muslims have been horrified by Bin Laden's command to kill civilians—an act flatly forbidden by the holy writings of Islam. But Bin Laden has repeatedly stated his belief that Islam is fighting a war of self-defense against enemies who, themselves, make no distinctions between soldiers and civilians. In a 1997 CNN interview with Peter Arnett, Bin Laden cited U.S. indifference to the April 18, 1996, massacre in Qana, Lebanon, in which Israeli rockets targeted a U.N. compound. In that attack 102 civilians were killed and many others wounded, including women and children. In the same interview, Bin Laden raised the memory of U.S. atomic bombs dropped on Hiroshima and Nagasaki in 1945, killing more than 100,000 civilians outright and causing many more deaths over time: "The U.S. does not consider it a terrorist act to throw atomic bombs at nations thousands of miles away, when it would not be possible for those bombs to hit military troops only. These bombs were rather thrown at entire nations, including women, children and elderly people and up to this day the traces of those bombs remain in Japan." Referring to an estimated 500,000 children who died prior to May 1996 because of U.S.-instigated UN sanctions against Iraq, Bin Laden added, "The U.S. does not consider it terrorism when hundreds of thousands of our sons and brothers in Iraq died for lack of food or medicine."[16] Bin Laden is convinced that a great double standard exists by which the United States and its allies are licensed to kill vast numbers of civilians while Muslims are condemned for much lesser attacks.

In addition to listing grievances, Bin Laden states simple goals for his jihad: He wants to drive Americans and Israelis out of the Middle East, overthrow non-Islamic governments in the region, abolish the corrupt Saudi monarchy, and ultimately create a caliphate—a pan-Islamic state. He even claims that he would end his war against America if it would drastically change its Middle East policies. "Your security is in your own hands," he said in his 2004 message to the American people. "And every state that doesn't play with our security has automatically guaranteed its own security."[17]

But such a statement may not indicate that America can hope to negotiate with Bin Laden or mollify him. For example, less than two years after the 9/11 attacks, the United States quietly began to remove its military bases from Saudi Arabia, thereby undoing the grievance that started Bin Laden's jihad in earnest. Bin Laden has never acknowledged this shift in U.S. policy, and his threats continue unabated.

INSURGENT, NOT TERRORIST

Nevertheless, the clarity of Bin Laden's thinking prompts some analysts to warn against too glibly labeling him a "terrorist." Michael Scheuer, who created and advised a secret CIA unit for tracking and eliminating Bin Laden, is especially adamant on this issue. He approvingly quotes British journalist Robert Fisk as saying that "'Terrorist' is a word that avoids all meaning."[18] According to Scheuer, the word conjures an image of a blood-crazed fanatic with no discernible goals or ideals. In Scheuer's words,

It was clear that bin Laden automatically was placed by the West's journalists and terrorism experts in the traditional terrorist category, where the only important issues are who or what bin Laden attacked, the method of attack, and how future attacks could be prevented. What bin Laden had been saying about why he and his al Qaeda forces were attacking was given short shrift.[19]

Whether or not one agrees with Scheuer's controversial assessment of Bin Laden as a "worthy enemy" who is "waging an insurgency, not a terrorist campaign,"[20] the CIA veteran argues persuasively that this unprecedented war America is fighting against al Qaeda is at least partly a war of language and ideas; it is essential to choose words carefully in order to achieve victory. To do so, Scheuer asserts that America and its leaders must fully understand Bin Laden's religious and intellectual groundings.

Bush discovered the perils of language soon after the attacks of 9/11. On September 16 he remarked, "This crusade, this war on terrorism is going to take a while."[21] Because Westerners routinely think of a crusade as a noble endeavor, the president did not consider the explosive connotations of that word in the Islamic world. Even moderate Muslims commonly associate the word *crusade* with atrocities committed by Europeans during the Middle Ages as they tried to seize Christian holy places from Islamic control. Bush's declaration of a *crusade* caused many Muslims to fear the onslaught of a religious war.

Bush hastened to correct his semantic error, immediately assuring Muslims everywhere that the coming war on terror would not be a war against Islam. "The face of terror is not the true faith of Islam," the president said the day after his "crusade" remark. "That's not what Islam is all about. Islam is peace. These terrorists don't represent peace. They represent evil and war."[22]

In his fatwas, interviews, and public statements, Bin Laden uses the words *crusade* and *crusaders* frequently—and always with a note of accusation. To him, America's war on terror and other actions in the Islamic world are simply continuations of the hated Christian Crusades of the Middle Ages. He repeatedly asserts that the Christian West, allied with Israel, intends nothing less than the complete annihilation of Islamic civilization, which has already fallen upon bad times.

A keen and well-read student of Islamic faith and history, Bin Laden is painfully aware that Islam, once one of the world's great cultures and religions, has suffered terrible humiliations during the last century. He dates the beginning of Islam's current crisis to the fall of the Ottoman Empire in 1922 (which, in his view, ended the original caliphate). After that, European powers divided up the Islamic world into largely artificial nation-states that have been weakened and exploited by the West ever since.

BIN LADEN'S CONCEPT OF JIHAD

Few historians—Western or Islamic—would quarrel with Bin Laden's belief that the twentieth-century breakup of the Muslim world was a disaster in the history of Islam. Bin Laden dreams of restoring Islamic glory through the creation of a single, unified Islamic state. According to the scholar-warrior Abdullah Azzam, one of Bin Laden's intellectual heroes and a comrade in arms during the Soviet-Afghan War, this caliphate would be extraordinarily vast, ranging from the Philippines in the east to Andalusia (southern Spain) in the west. Building such a huge nation-state ruled by a single caliph would require a massive jihad, and Bin Laden believes himself to be a humble part of this effort.

In addition to Azzam, Bin Laden's principal religious and political influences include the medieval theologian Ibn Taymiyah, who inspired the Wahhabite form of Islam under which Bin Laden was raised, and the twentieth-century Egyptian scholar Sayyid Qutb, author of the militant Islamist tract *Milestones* (also known as *Signposts Along the Road*). Azzam, Taymiyah, and Qutb impressed Bin Laden with a single guiding idea: the obligation of every Muslim male to take up jihad in defense of Islam.

Jihad, however, is a concept with many connotations, and Bin Laden's interpretation of it is controversial in the Islamic world. The prophet Muhammad himself spoke of two different kinds of jihad (again, meaning "effort" or "struggle"). Inner jihad is a spiritual struggle against one's own sins and frailties, an effort to become a better person and draw closer to God. Outer jihad is physical combat in defense of Islam. Muhammad made it clear that inner jihad is the "greater jihad," to be acted upon every day of an individual's life, while outer jihad is the "lesser jihad," to be acted upon only when the faith is under threat.

Bin Laden and other Islamist militants have persuaded many Muslims that Islam is, indeed, under threat from the Western world, and that militant jihad is a profound obligation. However, learned Muslims have accused Bin Laden of reversing the prophet's own teachings by regarding outer, militant jihad as greater than inner, spiritual jihad. M.A. Ashraf, an expert in al Qaeda doctrine and Islamic teachings, describes Bin Laden's understanding of jihad and Islam itself as deeply flawed:

> Whilst a Jihad aimed at restoring the freedom of conscience is an obligation in Islam, it does not eclipse the greater Jihad of the struggle between man and his ego. The *Hadith* [the body of writings about Muhammad's sayings and doings] records the Prophet after returning from a battle as saying to his followers "we must now return to the greater Jihad against one's ego." This is achieved through worship, the primary means of which is through the five daily congregational prayers—something that the Prophet never allowed to slip even during intense combat.

Ashraf adds that Bin Laden's comments about jihad "betray a distinct weakness in religious knowledge and reveal his subordination of spiritual enlightenment (the primary purpose of religion) to political prowess."[25]

In addition to criticisms from Ashraf and other Islamic scholars, there are further signs of tension between Bin Laden and the world's Muslims. On March 11, 2005, the Islamic Commission of Spain marked the first anniversary of deadly terrorist bombings in Madrid by issuing a legitimate fatwa against Bin Laden and al Qaeda. This document was signed by the commission's secretary general Mansur Escudero Bedate and was reportedly upheld by Islamic authorities in three North African nations. The fatwa denounces terrorism as incompatible with Islam and accuses Bin Laden of the crime of *istihlal*—making up one's own laws. Declaring that Bin Laden and other terrorists have excommunicated themselves from the religion of Islam, the document calls it "the duty of every Muslim . . . to fight actively against terrorism, in accordance with the Koranic mandate that establishes the obligation to prevent corruption from overtaking the Earth."[24]

BIN LADEN AFTER 9/11

Thus Bin Laden has placed himself at odds not only with the Western world but with mainstream Islam. Moreover, since the attacks of 9/11 he has demonstrated that his judgment is not infallible. The fall of the Soviet Union after the Soviet-Afghan War led him to believe that Islamist militants could easily destroy the world's remaining superpower, the United States. This belief was bolstered in the early 1990s, when Bin Laden aided attacks against U.S. troops facilitating humanitarian efforts in Somalia, causing the U.S. to withdraw its forces in 1994.

Consequently, after the attacks of 9/11, Bin Laden felt unduly safe from the United States under the Taliban's protection in Afghanistan. But in October 2001, U.S.- led forces invaded Afghanistan, and within a few months the Taliban government collapsed. Al Qaeda's military commander, Mohammed Atef, was killed during the fighting, and other al Qaeda leaders were killed or captured. For a short time after the fall of the Taliban, Bin Laden himself was suspected dead, either in fighting during the December 2001 Battle of Tora Bora or from natural causes. But evidence soon surfaced that al Qaeda's leader was alive and in hiding.

Even so, the defeat of Bin Laden and his organization seemed imminent to some analysts. Writing six months after the 9/11 attacks, Peter L. Bergen optimistically proposed that al Qaeda was doomed to perpetual decline:

> The defeat of the Taliban has important *long-term* implications because it does two things: it puts al-Qaeda's leadership on the run and it closes down the group's training camps in Afghanistan. Without the organizational skills of men like bin Laden and Ayman al-Zawahiri [Bin Laden's chief lieutenant], both of whom have been involved in planning paramilitary actions for decades, and the Afghan terror training camps, the group's ability to mount spectacular terrorist operations will diminish over time.[25]

However, not all analysts agree that the threat from Bin Laden and his ilk is waning. Michael Scheuer and Bergen himself acknowledge the continuing presence of several thousand al Qaeda agents throughout sixty countries. Middle East expert Benjamin Orbach has pointed out that such a sprawling, decentralized organization and the lack of a state sponsor are al Qaeda's strengths as well as its weaknesses, allowing it tremendous mobility and flexibility even while creating some operational difficulties. Al Qaeda, Orbach explains, can influence attacks by many other guerrilla organizations without directly planning or carrying out such attacks. Besides, as Michael Scheuer points out, guerrilla movements are notoriously tenacious and resilient: "In a guerrilla war . . . if the guerrilla force survives, it is winning."[26]

Moreover, the asymmetrical nature of al Qaeda's war against the West allows it to inflict great damage while suffering comparatively small loss of life and financial expense. For example, the attacks of 9/11 cost al Qaeda an estimated 200,000 to 500,00 dollars and the lives of 19 hijackers; the attacks cost the United States nearly 3,000 lives and hundreds of billions of dollars. In his videotaped October 2004 speech to the American people, Bin Laden cited such figures while stating his goal of bankrupting the United States.

An even more pressing concern is that al Qaeda will acquire—if it has not already—biological, chemical, or nuclear weapons. It is known that Bin Laden and his organization have been seeking such weapons since the late 1990s. Scheuer thinks it possible that al Qaeda has already obtained nuclear weapons small enough to be carried in suitcases. Bergen considers it likely that al Qaeda has acquired radioactive materials needed to make a so-called "dirty bomb"—a weapon which, if detonated in an urban area, would cause more panic than death. If Bin Laden and his followers possess such weapons, it is not surprising that they have not yet used them. Virtually all analysts agree that the al Qaeda leader is nothing if not patient; as the years of planning behind the 9/11 attacks proved, he is capable of taking his time to produce maximum results. "Because bin Laden's organization views military actions as a means to change U.S. policy," Scheuer warns, "the next attack is likely to be bigger than the September 2001 attacks."[27]

THE HAZARDS OF FIGHTING A LEGEND

The foregoing information leaves many enigmas about Bin Laden unresolved—including the question of how the West can ultimately defeat him, or where he might be hiding. Actually, Bin Laden's current whereabouts are not a complete mystery. In October 2004 John Lehman, a member of the National Commission on Terrorist Attacks Upon the United States (the 9/11 Commission), asserted that Bin Laden was in South Waziristan, a region of Pakistan not fully under Pakistani control. Lehman said that it would be currently difficult for U.S. forces to kill or capture Bin Laden without destabilizing the government of Pakistani leader Pervez Musharraf. Lehman also warned that sending U.S. troops after Bin Laden might result in a Vietnam-like situation that America could not afford. "We'll get (bin Laden) eventually," Lehman said, "just not now."[28]

Soon after the attacks of 9/11, the U.S. government regarded capturing or killing Bin Laden as a simpler matter. When asked on September 17, 2001, if he wanted Bin Laden dead, President George W. Bush answered, "There's an old poster out west, as I recall, that said, 'Wanted: Dead or Alive.'"[29] In those days, many analysts agreed that Bin Laden's death would be a tangible victory in the war on terror. Regarding the fear that Bin Laden's death would make him a martyr in the eyes of Islamists everywhere, Bergen wrote in 2002:

> [T]he most obvious statement you can make about martyrs is that they are dead, and that would immediately make bin Laden less potent. Bin Laden's al-Qaeda occupies the space that exists somewhere in between a cult and a genuine mass movement. Cults usually disappear with the deaths of their leaders. . . . So too will "Bin Ladenism" eventually join what President Bush has called "history's unmarked grave of discarded lies."[30]

But an increasing number of experts worry about the implications of Bin Laden's martyrdom, for despite his logistical and administrative brilliance, his influence among radical Islamists may well be more as a symbol than as a planner. British journalist Robert Fisk suggests that the thousands of cassette recordings of Bin Laden's voice circulating throughout the Islamic world may be far more potent instigators to terror than any plans he actually undertakes. And some analysts—including international relations scholar John Arquilla and CIA veteran Milt Bearden—warn that Bin Laden's death would grant him a legendary status that would make him more dangerous than ever.

Bearden has likened Bin Laden to Che Guevara, the Latin American Marxist revolutionary who helped Fidel Castro come to power in Cuba in 1959, then tried to foment revolutions in Africa and South America. Like Bin Laden, Guevara was a brilliant leader and tactician; but his violent death in 1967 turned him into something more—a worldwide legend. Almost four decades after his death, Guevara remains an inspiration to guerrilla insurgents everywhere, and his face appears on T-shirts and posters all over the world. Bearden warns that Bin Laden could acquire the same legendary charisma if he dies a violent death. As journalist Steve LeVine put it, "One Che was enough."[51]

The West must therefore consider carefully how Bin Laden and his movement can be decisively and finally defeated. There is a growing consensus among experts across the Western political spectrum—ranging from British journalist Robert Fisk on the left to CIA veteran Michael Scheuer on the right—that the war against Bin Laden must be fought with more than military force; it must also be fought with insight, imagination, and vision.

NOTES

1. *CNN.com*, "New Information Points to Bin Laden," September 12, 2001. http://edition.cnn.com/2001/US/09/11/investigation.terrorism/index.html.

2. Bill Clinton, "President Clinton's Oval Office Remarks on Anti-terrorist Attacks," U.S. Department of State, August 20, 1998. http://usinfo.state.gov/is/Archive_Index/President_Clintons_Oval_Office_Remarks_on_Antiterrorist_Attacks.html.

3. Quoted in Jesse J. DeConto, "American Media Called Instruments of War Propaganda," *Portsmouth Herald*, December 12, 2002.

4. Quoted in Mary Anne Weaver, "The Real bin Laden," *The New Yorker*, January 24, 2000.

5. Yossef Bodansky, *Bin Laden: The Man Who Declared War on America*, New York: Prima, 1999, p. 3.

6. Benjamin Orbach, "Usama bin Ladin and Al-Qa'ida: Origins and Doctrines," *Middle East Review of International Affairs (MERIA) Journal*, December 2001. http://meria.idc.ac.il/journal/2001/issue4/jvol5no4in.html.

7. Orbach, "Usama bin Ladin and Al-Qa'ida."

8. Quoted in Jason Burke, "The Making of the World's Most Wanted Man," *Observer*, October 28, 2001.

9. Khalid Batarfi, "My Sweet, Kind Osama," *The Mail on Sunday*, December 23, 2001.

10. Peter L. Bergen, *Holy War, Inc.: Inside the Secret World of Osama bin Laden*. New York: Touchstone, 2002, p. 34.

11. David Plotz, "What Does Osama Bin Laden Want? Nothing We Have," *Slate*, September 13, 2001. http://slate.com/id/115404.

12. George W. Bush, "Address to a Joint Session of Congress and the American People," White House, September 20, 2001. www.whitehouse.gov/news/releases/2001/09/20010920-8.html.

13. Osama bin Laden, "Full Transcript of Bin Laden's Speech," *Al jazeera.net*, November 1, 2004. http://english.aljazeera.net/NR/exeres/79C6AF22-98FB-4A1C-B21F-2BC36E87F61F.htm.

14. Quoted in *Washingtonpost.com*, "Ladenese Epistle: Declaration of War," www.washingtonpost.com/ac2/wp-dyn?pagename= article&node=&contentId=A4342-2001Sep21.

15. Quoted in *Washingtonpost.com*, "Jihad Against Jews and Crusaders," www.washingtonpost.com/ac2/wp-dyn?pagename= article&contentId=A4993-2001Sep21&notFound=true.

16. Osama bin Laden, "Transcript of Osama Bin Ladin interview by Peter Arnett," Information Clearing House, www.informationclearinghouse.info/article7204.htm.

17. Bin Laden, "Full Transcript of bin Laden's Speech."

18. Quoted in Anonymous [Michael Scheuer], *Through Our Enemies' Eyes: Osama bin Laden, Radical Islam, and the Future of America.* Washington, DC: Brassey's, 2003, p. xvi.

19. Anonymous, *Through Our Enemies' Eyes*, p. xv.

20. Anonymous, *Through Our Enemies' Eyes*, pp. 11, 198.

21. George W. Bush, "Remarks by the President Upon Arrival," White House, September 16, 2001. www.whitehouse.gov/ news/releases/2001/09/20010916-2.html.

22. Quoted in White House, "'Islam Is Peace' Says President," September 17, 2001. www.whitehouse.gov/news/releases/2001/ 09/20010917-11.html.

23. M.A. Ashraf, "True Islamic Teachings Compared to Al-Qaeda's Doctrine," *Review of Religions*, April 2004.

24. Liza Sabater, trans., "Text of the Fatwa Declared Against Osama Bin Laden by the Islamic Commission of Spain," *Culturekitchen*, March 12, 2005. www.culturekitchen.com/archives /002868.html.

25. Bergen, *Holy War, Inc.*, p. 239.

26. Anonymous, *Through Our Enemies' Eyes*, p. 142.

27. Anonymous, *Through Our Enemies' Eyes*, p. 230.

28. Quoted in Jim Mohr, "Osama Hiding in Pakistan," *San Bernardino Sun*, October 22, 2004.

29. Quoted in White House, "Guard and Reserves 'Define Spirit of America,'" September 17, 2001. www.whitehouse.gov/news/ releases/2001/09/20010917-3.html.

30. Bergen, *Holy War, Inc.*, p. 241.

31. Steve LeVine, "Making A Symbol Of Terror," *Newsweek*, March 1, 1999.

CHAPTER 1

FROM PRIVILEGED SON TO HOLY WARRIOR

OSAMA BIN LADEN

Bin Laden's Boyhood

Jason Burke

Born in 1957, Osama bin Laden was a son of
Muhammad bin Laden, one of Saudi Arabia's richest
and most powerful men. Osama's early life was
marked by privilege, piety, and stern work ethic. Because his mother, the tenth or eleventh of Muhammad bin Laden's spouses, was a foreigner stigma-
tized as "the slave wife," Osama felt like an outsider
even among his many half brothers. Nevertheless,
Osama seemed to be a child of considerable
promise. In this excerpt from an article in the *Observer* (a British newspaper), journalist Jason Burke
describes young Osama bin Laden as a courteous,
confident boy who grew increasingly discontented
with his life of luxury. Burke is the author of the
book *Al-Qaeda: Casting a Shadow of Terror.*

In 1930, a powerfully built dockside labourer, six feet tall
and with one eye, decided there was more to life than load-
ing ships in the ports of his poverty-stricken native province
of Hadramaut in Yemen. He packed a bag, bought a place on
a camel caravan heading to the newly created kingdom of
Saudi Arabia, and set off on a thousand-mile trek to seek his
fortune.

The man, who would go on to father a terrorist sought by
the military might of the Western world, got his first job as a
bricklayer with Aramco—the Arabian-American oil company—earning a single Saudi riyal, about 10p [or about 20¢
U.S.], a day. He lived frugally, saved hard, invested well and
went into business himself. By the early 1950s Mohamed bin
Laden was employed in building palaces for the House of
Saud in Riyadh. He won the contracts by heavily undercut-
ting local firms. It was a gamble that paid off.

Bin Laden's big break came when a foreign contractor
withdrew from a deal to build the Medina-Jedda highway and

he took on the job. By the early Sixties he was a rich man—and an extraordinary one.

"He couldn't read or write and signed his name with a cross all his life, but he had an extraordinary intelligence," said a French engineer who worked with him in the Sixties. The engineer remembered that the former labourer never forgot his roots, always leaving home "with a wad of notes to give to the poor."

Such alms-giving is one of the fundamentals of Islam. Bin Laden senior was a devout man, raised in the strict and conservative Wahhabi strand of Sunni Islam. Later he was to boast that, using his private helicopter, he could pray in the three holiest locations of Islam—Mecca, Medina and the al-Aqsa mosque in Jerusalem—in a single day. Visiting the former two sites must have been especially satisfying, for it was the contract to restore and expand the facilities serving pilgrims and worshippers there that established the reputation of his company, confirmed its status as the in-house builders of the Saudi ruling clan and made him stupendously wealthy. Though at one stage he was rich enough to bail out the royal family when they fell on hard times, the tatty bag he had carried when he left the Yemen remained on display in the palatial family home. He was killed when his helicopter crashed in 1968.

"THE SON OF THE SLAVE"

Mohamed bin Laden had, in the words of the French engineer, "changed wives like you or I change cars." He had three Saudi wives, Wahhabis like their husband, who were more or less permanent. The fourth, however, was changed on a regular basis.

The magnate would send his private pilot all over the Middle East to pick up yet another bride. "Some were as young as 15 and were completely covered [in traditional robes and veils] from head to toe," the pilot's widow recently recalled. "But they were all exceptionally beautiful."

Bin Laden's mother, Hamida, was not a Saudi or a Wahhabi, but a stunningly beautiful, cosmopolitan, educated 22-year-old daughter of a Syrian trader. She shunned the traditional Saudi veil in favour of Chanel trouser suits and this, coupled with the fact that she was foreign, diminished her status within the family. She was Mohamed bin Laden's tenth or eleventh spouse, and was known as "the slave wife."

Mohamed bin Laden gave even his former wives a home at his palaces in Jedda and Hijaz. Hamida was still married to the millionaire when he died and so, amid a huge family and the solid gold statues, the ancient tapestries and the Venetian chandeliers, this is where Osama bin Laden, Mohamed's seventh son, "the son of the slave," grew up.

A Childhood of Discipline and Privilege

Born in 1957—the year 1377 of the Islamic calendar—he was 11 when his father died. He never saw much of him. A flavour of the bin Laden household comes from a document provided to the American ABC TV network in 1998 by "an anonymous source close to bin Laden." It offers unprecedented insights into Osama's childhood. "The father had very dominating personality. He insisted to keep all his children in one premises," it reads. "He had a tough discipline and observed all the children with strict religious and social code. At the same time, the father was entertaining with trips to the sea and desert," the document goes on. "He dealt with his children as big men and demanded them to show confidence at young age."

Brian Fyfield-Shayler, 69, gave the then 13-year-old bin Laden and 30 other privileged classmates attending al-Thagh school, an elite Western-style Saudi school in Jedda, four one-hour English lessons a week during 1968 and 1969. He described bin Laden as a "shy, retiring and courteous" boy who was unfailingly polite. "He was very courteous— more so than any of the others in his class. Physically, he was outstanding because he was taller, more handsome and fairer than most of the other boys. He also stood out as he was singularly gracious and polite, and had a great deal of inner confidence," said Fyfield-Shayler.

Bin Laden was "very neat, precise and conscientious" in his work. "He wasn't pushy at all. Many students wanted to show you how clever they were. But if he knew the answer to something he wouldn't parade the fact. He would only reveal it if you asked him."

Youthful Travels

In bin Laden's early teens there was little sign of the fanatic he would become. In 1971 the family went on holiday en masse to the small Swedish copper mining town of Falun. A smiling Osama—or "Sammy" as he sometimes called himself—was pictured, wearing a lime-green top and blue flares, leaning on a Cadillac.

Osama, then 14, and his older brother Salem had first visited Falun a year before, driving from Copenhagen in a Rolls-Royce flown in from Saudi Arabia. Oddly, they stayed at the cheap Astoria hotel, where the owner, Christina Akerblad, recalled them spending the days out "on business" and the evenings eating dinner in their rooms. "I remember them as two beautiful boys—the girls in Falun were very fond of them," she said. "Osama played with my two [young] sons."

Akerblad remembered the wealth she found on display when cleaning the boys' rooms. "At the weekends we saw they used the extra bed in their rooms to lay out their clothes. They had lots of white silk shirts packaged in cellophane. I think they had a new one for every day—I never saw the dirty ones. They also had a big bag for their jewellery. They had emeralds and rubies and diamond rings and tie pins."

Nor was there any sign of incipient fervour in a bucolic summer at an Oxford language school in the same year. Bin Laden and his brothers befriended a group of Spanish girls and went punting on the Thames [in London].

Last month one woman showed a Spanish newspaper a photo of herself and girlfriends—one in hotpants—with three bin Laden boys. Bin Laden, wearing flares, a short-sleeved shirt and a bracelet, looks like any other awkward teenager. His two older brothers look more assured. The young Saudi even once stayed on London's Park Lane. He had forgotten the name of the hotel his Saudi parents had checked into, he told a reporter several years ago, but he recalled "the trees of the park and the red buses."

CHANGING VALUES

Quite how much of a personal fortune bin Laden had inherited is uncertain. It may well be a lot less than the huge sums (up to $250 million) often cited. The young bin Laden was never interested in money for its own sake. In fact, the very things that had made the father huge riches had begun to trouble the son. The early Seventies were a time of huge cultural change in the Middle East. Oil revenue, the wars with Israel and, above all, increasing contact with the West forced a profound re-examining of old certainties. For most of Mohamed bin Laden's numerous progeny, the answer lay in greater Westernisation and the elder members of the family set off for Victoria College in Alexandria in Egypt, Harvard, London or Miami. But not bin Laden. Like tens of thousands of other young men in the region at the time, Osama had become increasingly drawn to the cool, clear, uncluttered certainties of extremist Islamist ideology.

Young Bin Laden Turns to Islamism

Yossef Bodansky

Like many Saudi youths, Osama bin Laden was profoundly affected by events in the Arabic world during
the 1970s. It was a time of upheaval that brought the
assassination of Saudi Arabia's King Faisal, a peace
agreement between Israel and Egypt, the founding of
an Islamic republic in Iran, and the seizure of Mecca's
Grand Mosque by Muslim fundamentalists. In the following excerpt from his book *Bin Laden: The Man
Who Declared War On America*, Yossef Bodansky describes how such events molded Bin Laden's outlook.
As Bodansky implies, by late 1979, Bin Laden lacked
only a cause to put his newly found religious and political fervor into action. Bodansky is a former director
of the U.S. Congressional Task Force on Terrorism
and Unconventional Warfare; his other books include
Target America and the West: Terrorism Today and *The
Secret History of the Iraq War*.

Osama was destined to follow in his father's footsteps. He
went to high school in Jedda and then studied management
and economics at King Abdul Aziz University in Jedda, one
of Saudi Arabia's best schools. His father [Muhammad bin
Laden] promised him he would be put in charge of his own
company, which would enjoy the bin Ladens' direct access
to the [Royal] Court to gain extremely profitable contracts.

Osama bin Laden started the 1970s as did many other
sons of the affluent and well-connected—breaking the strict
Muslim lifestyle in Saudi Arabia with sojourns in cosmopolitan Beirut. While in high school and college Osama
visited Beirut [Lebanon] often, frequenting flashy nightclubs, casinos, and bars. He was a drinker and womanizer,
which often got him into bar brawls.

Ultimately, however, Osama bin Laden was not an ordinary Saudi youth having a good time in Beirut. In 1973 Muhammad bin Laden was deeply affected spiritually when he rebuilt and refurbished the two holy mosques, and these changes gradually affected Osama. Even while he was still taking brief trips to Beirut, he began showing interest in Islam. He started reading Islamic literature and soon began his interaction with local Islamists. In 1975 the outbreak of the Lebanese civil war prevented further visits to Beirut. The Saudi Islamists claimed that the agony of the Lebanese was a punishment from God for their sins and destructive influence on young Muslims. Osama bin Laden was strongly influenced by these arguments.

TURMOIL AND CHANGE

The drastic personal change in Osama bin Laden's life in the mid-1970s reflects the turmoil of the Arab Middle East, specifically Saudi Arabia, during the 1970s.

What began as a period of Arab self-respect and great expectations—derived from the self-perceived restoration of "Arab honor" in the 1973 Yom Kippur War (the coordinated Egyptian-Syrian surprise attack against Israel that ended with an inconclusive Israeli military victory) and then the great affluence and influence resulting from the oil boom that followed the embargo of 1973–1974 (which the oil-producing states of the Arabian Peninsula declared in order to force the West into adopting anti-Israeli policies)—quickly turned into an era of acute crisis and trauma due to the Arab world's inability to cope with the consequences of its actions. The sudden increase in wealth of the ruling elite and the upper and educated strata and exposure to the West led to confusion and a largely unresolved identity crisis resulting in radicalism and eruptions of violence. Improved media access and availability throughout the region brought home crises in other parts of the world. Because of its conservative Islamic character and sudden wealth and influence, Saudi Arabia was uniquely influenced by these dynamics.

ISLAMIST INTELLECTUALS AND WESTERN INFLUENCES

In Jedda, Osama bin Laden was constantly exposed to the often contradictory trends influencing Saudi society at the time. As Saudi Arabia's main port city on the Red Sea coast, Jedda was exposed to Western influence more than most other Saudi cities were. Sailors and experts came to Jedda, while the increasingly rich local elite, including the bin Laden family, visited the West. Coming from generally conservative and isolated Saudi Arabia, these visitors were shocked by their encounter with the West—by the personal freedoms and affluence of the average citizen, by the promiscuity, and by the alcohol and drug use of Western youth. Many young Saudis could not resist experimenting with the forbidden. When they returned to Saudi Arabia, they brought with them the sense of individualism and personal freedoms they encountered in the West.

The wealth and worldly character of Jedda also transformed it into a shelter for Islamist intellectuals persecuted throughout the Muslim world. Several universities, primarily King Abdul Aziz University in Jedda, which bin Laden attended from 1974 to 1978, became a hub of vibrant Islamist intellectual activity; the best experts and preachers were sheltered in the universities and mosques, providing an opportunity to study and share their knowledge. They addressed the growing doubts of the Saudi youth. Their message to the confused was simple and unequivocal—only an absolute and unconditional return to the fold of conservative Islamism could protect the Muslim world from the inherent dangers and sins of the West.

In March 1975, in the midst of the oil boom and the Islamic intellectual backlash against it, Saudi Arabia's King Faisal was assassinated. The assassin, Prince Faisal ibn Musaid, was the king's deranged nephew. He was also thoroughly Westernized and had visited the United States and Western Europe frequently. Both Islamists and Court insiders expressed apprehension that exposure to Western ways had caused Faisal ibn Musaid to go insane. Although the succession process worked and the kingdom suffered no ensuing crisis, the seed of doubt and discontent was sown. The assassination was a turning point for Saudi Arabia. For both the Saudi establishment and the conscientious elite, the assassination of the beloved king served as proof that the Islamists' warning against the sinful and perilous influence of the West had been on target. The shock of the assassination brought home the real and communal ramifications of the Westernization of the country's educated and affluent youth, creating a grassroots backlash and sending many of these youth, including bin Laden, back into the fold of Islamism.

EGYPT AND ANWAR SADAT

In the mid-1970s unfolding events in Egypt—the undisputed leader of the Arab world and politics—were also having a major impact on the Saudi educated elite. Jedda was the key entry port for printed material arriving from Egypt, and many of the Islamist intellectuals operating in the city's universities and mosques were Egyptian. They maintained close contacts with their colleagues still in Egypt and advocated their views, exposing the students of Jedda's universities, including bin Laden, to their works and opinions. Already attuned to and tilting toward Islamism, bin Laden was influenced by these Egyptian studies and the events that prompted them.

In the mid-1970s Egyptian president Anwar Sadat courted the Americans to gain political and economic assistance in working out a series of interim agreements with Israel. In

BIN LADEN'S FORM OF ISLAM

Osama bin Laden was raised in the Wahhabist form of Islam, and his religious beliefs continue to shape his actions today. In the following excerpt from an article in The New York Times, *journalist Neil MacFarquhar describes some of the beliefs of Wahhabism.*

The faith that drives Osama bin Laden and his followers is a particularly austere and conservative brand of Islam known as Wahhabism, which was instrumental in creating the Saudi monarchy. . . .

Throughout the sect's history, the Wahhabis have fiercely opposed anything they viewed as *bida,* an Arabic word, usually muttered as a curse, for any change or modernization that deviates from the fundamental teachings of the Koran.

The telephone, radio broadcasts and public education for women were at one point condemned as innovations wrought by the Devil. Riots ensued over the introduction of television in 1965, and were only quelled after police fired on demonstrators. Similar tensions exist today. A recent ruling suggested that the music played as mobile phone rings should be outlawed on religious grounds.

Whenever the forces of change prevailed, it was usually with the argument that the novelty could help propagate the Koran. When that argument fell flat, change stalled. So, for example, there are no movie theaters in Saudi Arabia—they the process of courting the United States, Sadat's image changed from that of a traditional village leader to that of a thoroughly Westernized world leader. The personality cult that Sadat developed domestically only alienated the educated elite, whose knowledge of and firsthand experience with the West caused them to fear its adverse impact on the traditional values of Muslim society.

THE PARTY OF GOD AND THE PARTY OF SATAN

The Islamist fundamentalist movement in Egypt was rejuvenated in the mid-1970s by young activists with Western— mainly secular and technical—educations who gave up their attempt to define their communal place in a world dominated by the West and its values. Intellectually active and curious, they produced high-quality literature that was widely circulated among the young Arab elite. In 1975 Egyptian writer and engineer Wail Uthman, one of the early influen-

---

would promote the unhealthy mingling of the sexes—and women are banned from driving.

But above all, the Wahhabis believe their faith should spread, not giving ground in any place they have conquered. . . .

The ferocity with which the Wahhabis fight for their cause is legend. One Arab historian described followers of the sect, founded in the 18th century, as they engaged in battle: "I have seen them hurl themselves on their enemies, utterly fearless of death, not caring how many fall, advancing rank with only one desire—the defeat and annihilation of the enemy. They normally give no quarter, sparing neither boys nor old men.". . .

Their Islam is an ascetic one. Men should wear short robes and even avoid the black cords used on head clothes. Mosques should be without decoration. There should be no public holidays other than religious ones, and even the prophet's birthday should not be celebrated. Drinking alcohol is forbidden.

Punishment should be meted out as described in the Koran. The right hand should be amputated for theft. Adulterers should be stoned to death. Murder and sexual deviation merit beheading. To this day Saudi Arabia carries out these punishments, especially beheading for capital crimes.

Neil MacFarquhar, "A Nation Challenged: Teachings; Bin Laden and His Followers Adhere to an Austere, Stringent Form of Islam," *The New York Times*, October 7, 2001.

tial ideologues of the most militant branch of the Islamist movement, published *The Party of God in Struggle with the Party of Satan.* This book divided the world into two social entities—the Party of God and the Party of Satan—and urged believers to fight to restore the rule of the former. In the preface to the second edition of his book, Uthman emphasized that in writing about the unbelievers, the members of the Party of Satan, he was actually referring to Sadat's regime. "Many thought I meant the Communist party when I wrote the Devil's party," he admitted. But although according to Uthman the Communists are an "essential support" of the Party of Satan, to him they are not the source of evil. "The Party of Satan is that group of people who pretend to believe in Islam but in reality are Islam's first enemies," Uthman wrote. He considered exposure to Western everyday life the source of the mounting crisis of Islam and saw no solution but Islamic militancy.

The Arab world was jolted in 1977 when Sadat visited Jerusalem and began the process that would lead to signing a peace agreement with Israel. Sadat's recognition of Israel was the first overt breaking of the "taboo" the Jewish state constitutes—the widest common denominator in the Arab world other than Islam. In his 1996 book *Secret Channels,* Egyptian journalist and commentator Mohamed Heikal stressed that the Arab world is motivated by "a blend of fury and revulsion" toward Israel that the present "peace process" has yet to breach. The combination of a dread of Westernization and the breaking of the "taboo" pushed many Arabs to extremes. The grassroots rejection of the president-turned-pharaoh mobilized scores of youth throughout all of Egyptian society—from the affluent and educated to the poor villagers and slum dwellers, from members of the security services to outcasts in the desert—to seek Islamist solutions to the profound crises afflicting Egypt.

PROOF OF RIGHTEOUSNESS

Soon Islamist youth in Egypt and elsewhere had forceful proof of the righteousness of their cause. On February 1, 1979, Ayatollah Ruhollah Khomeini returned to Iran, overthrew the shah, and established the Islamic Republic. Throughout the Muslim world the masses celebrated the success of Khomeini's Islamic Revolution as the triumph of Islam over the United States and the West. The Islamic Revolution became a source of pride and envy to all Muslims, as well as living proof that local rulers could be overthrown by Islamist forces. The impact of Iran was strong in Egypt because Sadat invited the deposed shah to take shelter there, a flagrant affront to the sentiments of most of the population.

The radical Shiite movement was the force behind the Iranian Revolution, and its development in Iran, Lebanon, and Iraq was almost simultaneous to and paralleled the evolution of Sunni revivalism in Egypt. By the late 1970s the philosophy of the revolutionary Shiite thinkers, as expressed in their writings, was very similar to that of the radical Sunni standard-bearers. Their approach to the diagnosis and cure of contemporary problems and their emphasis on the singular importance of confrontation and struggle were virtually identical. Saudi Arabia, in the middle, was exposed to the mounting Islamist fervor.

ASSAULT ON MECCA

Saudi Arabia was the first of the traditionalist conservative states to erupt in Islamist violence. On November 20, 1979, the Grand Mosque in Mecca was seized by a well-organized group of 1,300 to 1,500 men under the leadership of Juhayman ibn-Muhammad ibn-Sayf al-Utaibi. A former captain in the White Guards (National Guard), he now declared himself a "mahdi" (messiah). In addition to the Saudis the group's core included well-trained mujahideen (Islamic holy warriors) from Egypt, Kuwait, Sudan, Iraq, North Yemen (the YAR), and South Yemen (the PDRY). Egyptian and Soviet sources estimated the total number of rebels to be 3,500. Although the assault was in the name of the return to the purity of Islam, most of the 500 leading attackers had been trained and equipped in Libya and especially South Yemen by instructors from East Germany, Cuba, and the PFLP (Popular Front for the Liberation of Palestine). These attackers included Communists in command positions who demonstrated excellent organizational and tactical skills. Furthermore, fifty-nine of the participating Yemenis had been trained in Iran and received weapons via the Iranian Embassy in Sana.

During the preparations for the assault Juhayman's men had recruited several members of the elite White Guards and received active support in the smuggling of weapons and equipment into Saudi Arabia and the mosque itself. A White Guards colonel was among the senior instigators of the plot and organized the smuggling of the automatic weapons, provisions, and supplies into the mosque. The bulk of the weapons used had been brought from South Yemen over a lengthy period. The rebels also smuggled in huge quantities of food and drinking water to supply themselves and their supporters for a long siege.

On November 20, after a brief firefight to secure control of the Qaaba (the center of the Grand Mosque complex, containing the holiest shrine of Islam), Juhayman addressed the crowd of trapped pilgrims and asked for their support. Sermons and discussions of corruption, wastefulness, and the pro-Western stance of the Saudi royal family quickly gained the rebels widespread support among the worshipers. Before long most of the 6,000 pilgrims taken hostage asked to be issued arms so that they could join the revolt. Juhayman's sermons gained sympathy even among the leftist and quasi-Marxist students. News of Juhayman's sermons incited militant mobs throughout Saudi Arabia to storm local mosques and government posts. Latent subversive elements came to life as almost simultaneously with the seizure of the Qaaba a series of bombs exploded in places sensitive to the royal family in Mecca, Medina, Jeddah, and Riyadh. Among these targets were palaces, personal and official offices, and businesses.

Initially the White Guards reacted chaotically to the attack and suffered a humiliating defeat. Moreover, growing discontent in the ranks of the Saudi elite units led the royal family to fear that even they might rebel. The Saudi security forces settled for a siege of the mosque that lasted about two weeks. In the end the rebellion was only subdued by a special detachment of French paramilitary special forces, antiterrorist experts who used stun grenades and chemical weapons.

The uprising in Mecca shook the world of accepted norms in Saudi Arabia. The grievances raised by Juhayman echoed throughout Saudi Arabia, being whispered about in closed meetings. In intellectual circles his arguments made people stop and think about Islam and the society they were living in. A thinking and well-read individual, Osama bin Laden was influenced by the social issues Juhayman raised. But although the crisis of November 1979 reinforced bin Laden's conviction that only an Islamic government could shield Saudi Arabia and the rest of the Muslim world from the evils of encroaching Westernization, he remained a loyal subject of King Fahd and the House of al-Saud.

Finding a Cause in the War Against the Soviets

Peter L. Bergen

Osama bin Laden's life finally found purpose during the last days of 1979, when the Soviet Union invaded Afghanistan. For several years, Bin Laden traveled between Saudi Arabia and the Afghan-Pakistani border, assisting the Muslim, anti-Soviet mujahideen (holy warriors) with money, machinery, and recruits. In 1987, Bin Laden had his first combat experience in the battle of Jaji, where his battlefield exploits inaugurated his transformation into an Arab folk hero. When the Soviets left Afghanistan in 1989, Bin Laden felt that he and his comrades had been instrumental in defeating a superpower. In the following excerpt from his book *Holy War, Inc.*, Peter L. Bergen relates Bin Laden's activities during the Soviet-Afghan war, explaining how the conflict led to his founding of al Qaeda in 1989. Bergen is CNN's terrorism analyst. His articles have appeared in the *New Republic*, *Vanity Fair*, and other publications.

Within weeks of the Soviet invasion [of Afghanistan in December 1979], bin Laden, then twenty-two, voted with his feet and wallet, heading to Pakistan to meet with the Afghan leaders Burhanuddin Rabbani and Abdul Rasool Sayyaf, whom he had previously encountered during Hajj [pilgrimage to Mecca] gatherings. He then returned to Saudi Arabia and started lobbying his family and friends to provide money to support the Afghan guerrillas and continued making short trips to Pakistan for his fund-raising work.

SETTING TO WORK IN AFGHANISTAN

In the early 1980s bin Laden, already an expert in demolition from time spent working in his family's construction

Peter L. Bergen, *Holy War, Inc.: Inside the Secret World of Osama bin Laden*. New York: Touchstone, 2002. Copyright © 2001 by Peter L. Bergen. All rights reserved. Reproduced by permission of Touchstone, an imprint of Simon & Schuster Macmillan.

business, made his first trips into Afghanistan, bringing with him hundreds of tons of construction machinery, bulldozers, loaders, dump trucks, and equipment for building trenches, which he put at the disposal of the *mujahideen.* The machinery would be used to build rough roads, dig tunnels into the mountains for shelter, and construct rudimentary hospitals. Bin Laden's followers also set up mine-sweeping operations in the Afghan countryside.

Despite the fact that the United States was also supporting the *mujahideen,* bin Laden was already voicing anti-American sentiments during the early eighties. Khaled al-Fawwaz, bin Laden's London contact, recalls his friend saying in 1982 that Muslims should boycott American products. In a 1999 interview, Bin Laden himself said that during the mid-1980s he gave lectures in Saudi Arabia urging attacks on U.S. forces and the boycott of American products.

In 1984 bin Laden set up a guesthouse in Peshawar [Pakistan] for Muslims drawn to the jihad. It was called *Beit al-Ansar,* or House of the Supporters, an allusion to the Prophet Muhammad's followers who helped him when he had to flee his native Mecca for Medina. Initially the house was simply a way station for those who would be sent for training with one of the Afghan factions. Later, bin Laden would form his own military operation. At about the time bin Laden founded Beit al-Ansar, his former professor Abdullah Azzam established the *Mekhtab al-Khadamat,* or Services Office, in Peshawar. The Services Office started publishing reports about the Afghan war and engaged in a global campaign to recruit Muslims for the jihad. Bin Laden was its principal funder. Eventually there would [be] a dozen or so guesthouses in Peshawar under the aegis of the Services Office.

THE INFLUENCE OF OLDER MEN

Azzam was both the ideological godfather and the global recruiter par excellence of Muslims drawn to the Afghan jihad; he would exert a strong pull on bin Laden by virtue of his Islamic credentials and greater experience of the world. According to the Palestinian journalist Jamal Ismail, who was a student in Peshawar during the 1980s and met with bin Laden repeatedly after 1984: "It was Azzam who influenced Osama to finance the Arab fighters who came to Afghanistan." In an interview with an Arabic-language television station, bin Laden himself describes Azzam as "a man worth a nation." Those who knew Azzam and bin Laden during this period recall that while Azzam was eloquent and charismatic, bin Laden, then in his mid-twenties, seemed sincere and honest but not a potential leader.

Having lost his deeply religious father while he was still a child, bin Laden would, throughout his life, be influenced by religiously radical older men—first, Azzam and, to a lesser extent, the Afghan commander Abdul Rasool Sayyaf; later, the second-in-command in his jihadist organization, Ayman al-Zawahiri. All of these men had a very definite vision of how to conduct a life devoted to holy war. But bin Laden clearly sees his father as the ultimate inspiration for his jihad. He has told a Pakistani journalist: "My father was very keen that one of his sons should fight against the enemies of Islam. So I am the one son who is acting according to the wishes of his father."...

A barrel-chested man whose enormous gray beard and fiery rhetoric made him a commanding presence, Azzam believed that jihad was an absolute necessity to restore the *Khalifa*, the dream that Muslims around the world could be united under one ruler. His motto was "Jihad and the rifle alone: no negotiations, no conferences and no dialogues." And he put that belief in practice, often joining the *mujahideen*, "holy warriors," battling the Soviets in Afghanistan.

THE DUTY OF JIHAD

For Azzam the jihad in Afghanistan was an *obligation* for every Muslim, as he explained in a widely distributed pamphlet entitled "Defending Muslim Territory Is the Most Important Duty." And it was not simply from Afghanistan that the infidels had to be expelled. Azzam wrote: "This duty will not end with victory in Afghanistan; jihad will remain an individual obligation until all other lands that were Muslim are returned to us so that Islam will reign again: before us lie Palestine, Bokhara, Lebanon, Chad, Eritrea, Somalia, the Philippines, Burma, Southern Yemen, Tashkent and Andalusia [southern Spain]."

Azzam traveled all over the world to recruit men and money for the Afghan jihad, preaching that "to stand one hour in the battle line in the cause of Allah is better than sixty years of night prayer." Khaled al-Fawwaz recalls that Azzam was a one-man "wire service" for the jihad movement, traveling to Kuwait, Yemen, Bahrain, Saudi Arabia, and the United States to gather and spread news, recruit men, and raise millions of dollars for the cause. . . .

Azzam was often seen in the company of the Egyptian militant Sheikh Rahman in Peshawar. Rahman also founded a guesthouse in the city, traveling there at least twice during the 1980s. In 1985, Rahman made his first trip into Afghanistan under the aegis of the ultra-Islamist Afghan leader Gulbuddin Hekmatyar. The sheikh, who had been blinded by diabetes when he was a baby, wept as he heard the crashing of artillery shells in the distance, bemoaning the fact that he could not see for himself his dream of jihad in action.

SUPPORTERS AND FUNDERS

Another influential figure in the Arab effort to support the war was Muhammad Abdurrahman Khalifa, a Jordanian, who would later go on to marry one of bin Laden's sisters. Khalifa headed the Jordanian branch of the Muslim Brotherhood, which supplied recruits for the Afghan jihad. Khalifa also worked in Peshawar as head of the Saudi Muslim World League office during the Afghan jihad.

Meanwhile, bin Laden traveled back and forth to Saudi Arabia, bringing donations for various Afghan parties, including that of the military commander Ahmad Shah Massoud, a moderate Islamist. But bin Laden would form his closest ties with the ultra-Islamist Hekmatyar and with Abdul Rasool Sayyaf, an Afghan leader who was fluent in Arabic and had studied in Saudi Arabia. Sayyaf also subscribed to the purist Wahhabi Islam dear to bin Laden's heart. Because of his close ties to Arabia, Sayyaf would receive hundreds of millions of dollars in Saudi aid.

Afghan commanders in the field understood the importance of Arab funding. Peter Jouvenal, the British cameraman who traveled into Afghanistan dozens of times during the war against the Soviets, described visiting a base in Pakistan built during the early 1980s by Jalaluddin Haqqani: "He decided to build [it] so he could show off to Arab donors," Jouvenal recalled. "When I visited there were underground bunkers. You could have been inside a house. There was wallpaper, carpets, toilets, and a generator for electricity. The bunker I was in slept four people. It was built into a cliff. The complex was spread out over a five-kilometer radius. In 1982 I saw a raid by the Russians on the base. It lasted about ten minutes. Four or so planes dropped high explosives, but no one was killed. The base had its own PR department. They shot videos of executions of Russians and sent them to Saudi Arabia for fund-raising purposes." (This base would later be used by al-Qaeda in the 1990s.)

THE AFGHAN ARABS

With the establishment of the Services Office by Azzam and bin Laden in 1984, Arab support for the *mujahideen* became more overt. The recruits for the Afghan jihad came to be known as the Afghan Arabs. None of them was Afghan, and while most were Arabs, they also came from all over the Muslim world. Some of them were high school students who went on trips to the Afghan-Pakistan border that were not much more than the equivalent of jihad summer camp. Some were involved in support operations along the border, working for charities and hospitals. Others spent years in fierce battles against the communists.

According to the Palestinian journalist Jamal Ismail, three countries provided the lion's share of the Afghan Arabs: Saudi Arabia, Yemen, and Algeria. Saudi Arabia's national airline even gave a 75 percent discount to those going to the holy war. By Ismail's account, fifty thousand Arabs came to Peshawar to fight. Bin Laden's friend Khaled al-Fawwaz told me the figure was 25,000. Milt Bearden, who ran the CIA's Afghan operation between 1986 and 1989, also puts the figure at 25,000. No one really knows the exact figure, but it seems safe to say that the total number of Afghan Arabs who participated in the jihad over the course of the entire war was in the low tens of thousands.

It is worth noting here that the maximum combined strengths of the various Afghan *mujahideen* factions averaged somewhere between 175,000 and 250,000 in any given year. These numbers demonstrate that the Afghan Arabs' contribution to the war against the Soviets was insignificant from a military point of view. The war was won primarily with the blood of Afghans and secondarily with the treasure of the United States and Saudi Arabia, who between them provided approximately $6 billion in support.

LESSONS OF JIHAD

Of course, bin Laden and various other Afghan Arabs served as conduits for some of this money. Milt Bearden estimated that about $20 million a month was flowing into the Afghan jihad from Saudi sources after the summer of 1986. Prince Turki al-Faisal Saud, the head of the Saudi General Intelligence agency, managed the Saudi contribution, aided by Prince Salman, the governor of Riyadh. Bin Laden worked closely with Prince Turki during this period, effectively working as an arm of Saudi intelligence. In addition the Muslim World League, headed by the leading Saudi cleric Sheikh Abd al-Aziz bin Baz, provided funding. (It is ironic that billions of dollars of Saudi government aid helped create a cadre of well-trained militants who would later turn against the Saudi royal family. This is part of a continuing larger pattern of Saudi funding of militant Islamist organizations, known as riyalpolitik, which is supposed to shore up Saudi legitimacy, but actually undermines it, because it funds the very groups most opposed to the Saudi regime.)

Still, in the grand scheme of things the Afghan Arabs were no more than extras in the Afghan holy war. It was the lessons they learned from the jihad, rather than their contribution to it, that proved significant. They rubbed shoulders with militants from dozens of countries and were indoctrinated in the most extreme ideas concerning jihad. They received at least some sort of military training, and in some cases battlefield experience. Those who had had their tickets punched in the Afghan conflict went back to their home countries with the ultimate credential for later holy wars. And they believed that their exertions had defeated a superpower. "The Afghan jihad plays a central role in the evolution of the Islamist movement around the world," writes Gilles Kepel, a scholar of militant Islam. "It replaces the Palestinian cause in the Arab imagination, and symbolizes the movement from [Arab] nationalism to Islamism."

BIN LADEN'S BAPTISM BY FIRE

Jamal Ismail recalls that by about December 1984, bin Laden had become an important figure in the jihad effort. Around this time Azzam announced that bin Laden would pay the living expenses of the families of men who came to fight in the Afghan war. Since Pakistan was inexpensive, that sum was about $300 a month per family. Still, it added up. According to Essam Deraz, an Egyptian filmmaker who covered bin Laden in the late 1980s, the Saudi was subsidizing the Afghan Arabs at a rate of $25,000 a month during this period. Bin Laden's friend al-Fawwaz said bin Laden also started thinking about how he could create a mobile force. "He bought four-wheel-drive pickups and equipped every one with antitank missiles and mine detection so that each unit would be capable of dealing with any kind of situation," recounted al-Fawwaz in his London office.

In 1986 bin Laden moved to Peshawar permanently, directing his operation from a two-story villa in the suburb of University Town where he both worked and lived. It was at this time that bin Laden founded his first camp inside Afghanistan, named al-Ansar, near the village of Jaji in Paktia province, a few miles from a portion of Pakistan's North-West Frontier that juts into Afghanistan. At Jaji, bin Laden and his men would receive their baptism by fire: a week-long siege by the Soviets that has become a cornerstone of the popular legend surrounding bin Laden.

According to Deraz, who said he witnessed the battle of Jaji from a distance of about two miles, the Soviet assault began on April 17, 1987. The Arabs had based themselves at Jaji because it was close to the Soviet front lines, and had used bin Laden's construction equipment to dig themselves into caves in the heights around the village. For about a week they endured punishing bombardment by two-hundred-odd Russians, some of whom were wearing the uniform of Spetsnaz, Russia's special forces. Of about fifty Arabs, more than a dozen were killed before the group realized they could no longer hold their position and withdrew.

A HERO SUFFERS HEALTH PROBLEMS

Despite this retreat, Jaji was celebrated as a victory in the Arab world. It was the first time the Afghan Arabs had held their ground for any length of time against such superior forces. Arab journalists based in Peshawar wrote daily dispatches about bin Laden's battlefield exploits that were widely published in the Middle East and brought a flood of new recruits to the Afghan jihad. Osama, "the lion," was lionized for leaving behind the typical Saudi multimillionaire's life of palaces in Jeddah and hotel suites in London and Monte Carlo for the dangers of the war in Afghanistan. This was in sharp contrast to the thousands of members of the al-Saud ruling family, none of whom seem to have fought in Afghanistan despite awarding themselves the title of "Custodians" of Islam's holiest sites in 1986.

Another man who made his name at Jaji was Abu Ubaidah,

an Egyptian, who later drowned in a ferry accident in Kenya. The U.S. government indictment of bin Laden names Abu Ubaidah as his "ranking military commander" until his death in 1996.

If the battle of Jaji was dangerous, the rigors of daily life were nearly as taxing for bin Laden. In a slim Arabic biography published in 1991, Deraz wrote that bin Laden's health problems during this period forced him to lie down intermittently for hours at a time. He suffered from low blood pressure, which was treated by an Egyptian doctor from Peshawar, and diabetes, for which he received insulin shots. One of the photographs in the book shows bin Laden getting a shot after being exposed to "poisonous gas." Another shows bin Laden tending a wound in his foot.

A VIOLENT SPIRITUALITY

I met Deraz in Cairo in December 2000 to talk about bin Laden. . . . Deraz said he met bin Laden, who until that point had avoided journalists, in 1987. From their first encounter, which took place in Peshawar, Deraz says he told bin Laden that "one day you [the Afghan Arabs] are all going to prison." But bin Laden was unmoved. "He thought we would be like heroes [back home]. He did not understand that our [Middle Eastern] governments hate any kind of popular movement."

But bin Laden wasn't focusing on politics. For him, the Afghan war was an extraordinary spiritual experience. During his CNN interview he told us: "I have benefited so greatly from the jihad in Afghanistan that it would have been impossible for me to gain such a benefit from any other chance. . . . What we benefited from most was [that] the glory and myth of the superpower was destroyed not only in my mind, but also in [the minds] of all Muslims." So convinced was bin Laden of the spiritual greatness of the struggle he was undertaking that he asked his eldest son, Abdullah, then aged twelve, to visit him during the war.

Thousands of other Afghan Arabs were similarly moved. A case in point is Mansoor al-Barakati, a Saudi from Mecca, whose story is told on an Islamist Web site. Al-Barakati traveled to Afghanistan in 1987 to bring home a younger brother who had gone for jihad. When he crossed the border between Pakistan and Afghanistan he felt his "heart shake" with the feeling of entering a divine place. Giving up the search for his brother, al-Barakati traveled to Jalalabad, training at one of bin Laden's camps for two months. From there he moved to the deserts around Kandahar, which saw some of the worst fighting of the war. Al-Barakati distinguished himself by exceptional acts of heroism, rising to become the leader of the Arab *mujahideen* in the area. During the summer of 1990, a 120mm rocket hit the rooftop of a house on which al-Barakati was sitting. Bleeding heavily, he was driven to Pakistan for medical attention. On the way he pleaded for death, crying, "I am fed up with this worldly life. I really love Allah." Finally he died and, as in many accounts of the Arabs who are *shaheed*, "martyred," a witness recounted that a "beautiful scent the likes of which I have never experienced in my life" emanated from the body.

THE FOUNDING OF AL-QAEDA

The Afghan war did not only move men like bin Laden spiritually; it also enabled them to meet key figures in terrorist organizations in the Arab world. In 1987 bin Laden was introduced to members of Egypt's Jihad group, the organization behind the 1981 assassination of Egyptian President Anwar Sadat. A leader of the group, Ayman al-Zawahiri, had settled in Peshawar and was putting his skills as a physician to work at a hospital for Afghan refugees. In 1989, bin Laden founded al-Qaeda, "the base" in Arabic, an organization that would eventually merge with al-Zawahiri's Jihad group.

Jamal Ismail says al-Qaeda's initial goals were prosaic. Most Arabs continued to arrive under the umbrella of the Services Office and bin Laden's guesthouse, Beit al-Ansar, remained open to all comers. But there were concerns that Middle Eastern governments, worried about Islamist movements in their own countries, had penetrated these organizations, so al-Qaeda was formed as a more secure unit. "They had a separate guesthouse," Ismail recalled. "Unless you were part of the inner circle you could not enter this house."

The Saudi dissident Saad al-Fagih suggests yet another reason for the founding of al-Qaeda. In 1988, bin Laden realized that there was little documentation to give to the families of those missing in Afghanistan; to solve this problem, he set up al-Qaeda to track those who were full-fledged *mujahideen*, those who were involved only in charity work in Peshawar, and those who were simply visitors. Movements between the guesthouses and military training camps were also recorded. Al-Fawwaz says these documents were subsequently used by Middle Eastern governments to identify potential Islamist militants.

AL-QAEDA'S THIRD MEMBER

The fullest accounting of the founding of al-Qaeda comes from Jamal al-Fadl, the U.S. government's first witness at the New York trial of four bin Laden associates in 2001. Al-Fadl, a Sudanese then in his early twenties, fought with bin Laden's group on the Afghan front lines in 1989. He was also trained to shoot down helicopters and attended courses on the use of explosives. In 1989 he was approached to become part of al-Qaeda, which planned to continue holy wars beyond the Afghan conflict. He performed *bayat*, an oath of fealty, to the group's jihad agenda and signed papers indicating his allegiance to the *emir*, bin Laden. Al-Fadl was al-Qaeda's third member.

Al-Fadl defected after it was discovered that he had embezzled $110,000 from the organization, and he later became a U.S. government informant. At the Manhattan trial, al-Fadl outlined the operational structure of al-Qaeda and the responsibilities of various committees, among them the media operation, run by a man with the alias Abu Reuter.

In February 1989 the Soviets withdrew from Afghanistan and bin Laden turned his attention to other struggles. He returned to Jaji, a place that had assumed tremendous symbolic importance, and made it a base. Peter Jouvenal was in the area around that time. "I witnessed them digging huge caves, using explosives and Caterpillar digging equipment. I was told that I wasn't safe and should move on."

TARGETING A PAKISTANI LEADER

One of bin Laden's initial targets was the first woman to lead a modern Muslim nation: Pakistan's prime minister, Benazir Bhutto, regarded as a liberal because of her education at Oxford and Harvard. Bhutto's predecessor, the military dictator General Zia ul-Haq, had died in a mysterious plane crash the year before her election. Zia had been a strong supporter of Islamist groups in Pakistan, and these groups saw Bhutto as a threat.

I met with the former prime minister at a well-kept suburban New Jersey home just across the George Washington Bridge from Manhattan, on a dank, freezing day in March 2000. . . . "The first time I heard of Osama was in 1989 during a no-confidence vote against my government," she said. "Four parliamentarians came to me with briefcases of money. They had twelve and [a] half lakhs of rupees, about eighty to a hundred thousand dollars they had been given to vote against me. They said the money came from Saudi Arabia. I was shocked, because King Fahd was a supporter and had made a special effort to help my country. I sent a delegation to Saudi Arabia to ask why are the Saudis funding this." The reply, she said, was that "'there is a rich Saudi individual who is doing this, Osama bin Laden.' I had never heard of him. . . ."

"The international Islamist movement [that emerged out of the Afghan war] saw Pakistan as its base," she explained. "They saw my party as a liberal threat." On November 1, 1989, Bhutto narrowly survived the no-confidence vote.

A few weeks later, on November 24, bin Laden's mentor Abdullah Azzam was assassinated, a crime that remains unsolved. A car bomb planted at the entrance of the Saba-e-Leil Mosque in Peshawar exploded at midday as Azzam was going to Friday prayers. Also killed with him were two of his sons, Muhammad, twenty-three, and Ibrahim, fourteen.

By the end of 1989 there was little reason for bin Laden to linger in Pakistan. He was persona non grata with the new Pakistani government, the Soviets had withdrawn from Afghanistan, and his closest jihad collaborator was dead. So for the first time in several years he returned to live in his native country, where he would take up other holy wars.

He was thirty-two.

CHAPTER 2

BIN LADEN AND AL QAEDA

PEOPLE
WHO MADE
HISTORY

OSAMA BIN LADEN

Al Qaeda Under Bin Laden's Leadership

Benjamin Orbach

Al Qaeda, the name of Osama bin Laden's worldwide network, means "the base." It is an umbrella organization made up of some three thousand to five thousand followers, the stated goal of whom is to expel all non-Muslims from the Middle East. While al Qaeda has been directly responsible for some guerrilla attacks, it frequently serves to inspire and influence the deeds of other groups and individuals. It is therefore as much a symbol of Islamist unity and brotherhood as it is an organization. In the following excerpt from an article in *Middle East Review of International Affairs*, Benjamin Orbach discusses al Qaeda's doctrines, sources of income, and actions, while emphasizing Bin Laden's leadership role. Orbach is a fellow at the School of Advanced International Studies, Johns Hopkins University.

[Al-Qa'ida's] central principle is to expel the forces of unbelievers and heresy from the Middle East. Al-Qa'ida considers the United States and its allies, the region's "oppressive, corrupt, and tyrannical regimes," to be heretics that wage war against Muslims through murder, torture, and humiliation. Most offensive to bin Ladin and his followers is the U.S. "occupation of the land of the two Holy Places," Saudi Arabia.

THE CATASTROPHE OF U.S. PRESENCE

The 1998 "*fatwa*" of al-Qa'ida and its allies, the "Declaration of the World Islamic Front for Jihad against the Jews and the Crusaders," described the U.S. presence as a catastrophe that had humiliating and debilitating effects on the Muslim people. Bin Laden wrote, "Since God laid down the Arabian peninsula, created its desert, and surrounded it with its seas,

Benjamin Orbach, "Usama bin Ladin and Al-Qa'ida: Origins and Doctrines," *Middle East Review of International Affairs Journal*, vol. 5, December 2001. Copyright © 2001 by Global Research in International Affairs. Reproduced by permission.

no calamity has ever befallen it like these Crusader hosts that have spread in it like locusts, crowding its soil, eating its fruits, and destroying its verdure."

A Western power has never occupied the Hijaz [the region of the two Holy Places] in Muslim history. Traditionally, non-Muslims are not permitted to enter the Hijaz based on the Prophet's deathbed statement, "Let there not be two religions in Arabia." Historian Bernard Lewis explained that the sanctity of the Hijaz is clear from the disparate difference between the fall of Jerusalem to the Crusaders in 1099 and [Arabian leader] Saladin's attack on Reynald of Chatillon in 1182. In the case of Jerusalem, the Crusaders roused little interest in [the Islamic centers of] Damascus and Baghdad when they captured the city. In contrast, when Reynald attacked Muslim caravans in the Hijaz, including those of pilgrims to Mecca, his actions were perceived as a "provocation" and a "challenge directed against Islam's holy places." Saladin responded by declaring jihad upon the Crusaders.

More than eight hundred years later, bin Ladin applies the same principle and interprets the U.S. presence as an equal provocation requiring a similar solution. As retribution, bin Ladin anticipated "a black future for America. Instead of remaining [the] United States, it shall end up separated states and shall have to carry the bodies of its sons back to America." And in revenge for the Saudi regime's alleged betrayal of the Islamic people, bin Ladin expects the royal family to be expelled from the faith and to face a similar fate as that which befell the Shah of Iran.

AMERICAN AND ISRAELI CRIMES AGAINST ISLAM

After long emphasizing the U.S. presence in Saudi Arabia, bin Ladin moved to other issues dealing with the U.S. attempt to destroy Islam. These included an opposition to UN sanctions against Iraq [after the 1990 invasion of Kuwait] (which he blamed on the United States) as killing the Muslim Iraqi people and the assertion that the United States was supporting the Jews in an effort to "achieve full control over the Arab peninsula." Bin Ladin claimed the United States did not rest after the "slaughter" of the Gulf War but instead pushed for the "dismemberment and the destruction . . . of what remains of this people and to humiliate their Muslim neighbors." These actions, according to bin Ladin, are meant to divert attention from the Jewish occupation of Jerusalem and the killing of Muslims in Palestine. In a 1996 interview, bin Ladin outlined American and Israeli crimes against Islam from Iraq to Qana [Lebanon, during a 1996 massacre] to Bosnia [during the war of the early 1990s] and detailed the "killing [of] weaker men, women, and children in the Muslim world." To further demonstrate America's brutality, he cited the use of atomic weapons on Hiroshima and Nagasaki in non-Muslim Japan at the end of World War Two.

From bin Ladin's perspective, these attacks in Saudi Arabia, Iraq, and Palestine meant a declaration of war on God and the Prophet, making it Muslims' duty to fight a holy war "to glorify the truth and to defend Muslim Land, especially the Arab peninsula." More recently, he has also elevated the plight of Muslims in Kashmir, East Timor, and other places such as the Sudan, Somalia, and Chechnya to his list of top grievances. Bin Ladin believes that all Muslims need to pool their resources, stand together, and fight against the threat to Islam, acting as a unified nation that overcomes superficial, contrived national differences to fight against its common enemies.

In a sense, al-Qa'ida, an umbrella framework of groups committed to Jihad that acts together in recruiting, training, and planning of guerrilla actions, is a symbol of the goal. Like bin Ladin's vision for the future, al-Qa'ida crosses national boundaries through a bridge of Islamic brotherhood and a hatred for the United States and its allies. While each group and even different cells have local interests, they share a common enemy and a greater common goal. . . .

AL-QA'IDA'S LEADERSHIP

[Al-Qa'ida's other leaders include] Dr. Ayman al-Zawahiri and Sleiman Abu Gheith. Al-Zawahiri was leader of Egyptian Islamic Jihad, the group responsible for the 1981 assassination of [Egyptian president Anwar] Sadat, until 1998 when he signed the World Islamic Front's *fatwa* for Fighting Jews and Crusaders. This decision split the group since many members objected to diverting from its original focus of making an Islamist revolution in Egypt. After spending three years in an Egyptian prison, al-Zawahiri left Egypt for Pakistan, the Sudan, and then Afghanistan and vowed to return "a conqueror only." Due to his experience, al-Zawahiri is one al-Qa'ida's ideological authorities and a great influence on bin Ladin. He is associated with the 1995 bombing of the Egyptian embassy in Pakistan, for which he was sentenced to death by an Egyptian court, and the 1998 U.S. embassy bombings in Africa, for which a New York grand jury indicted him in 1999. Abu Gheith, a former imam at a government-backed mosque in Kuwait, has a more junior position in the organization as a spokesperson.

Two other important al-Qa'ida officials have been Muhammad Atef, reportedly killed in November 2001 by U.S. bombs in Afghanistan, and Abu Zubaydah. Atef was a former Egyptian police officer who, like al-Zawahiri, had roots in Egyptian Islamic Jihad. He was al-Qa'ida's military commander in charge of recruiting and training militants, and was suspected of involvement in the Somalia operations in the early 1990s and the planning of the U.S. embassy bombings in Africa. Abu Zubaydah, born in Saudi Arabia but of Palestinian origin, is also involved in recruiting. He brought in Ahmad Ressam and played a role in the proposed millennial bombings. A Jordanian court sentenced him to death in absentia in 2000.

Under this leadership, al-Qa'ida, which means "the base," is an umbrella organization with an estimated 3000 to 5000 followers that works in conjunction with Islamic Jihad and Gamaa Islamiya in Egypt, Harak ul-Ansar in Pakistan, and has contacts with the National Islamic Front in the Sudan. The group's intention was to take *mujahideen* [holy warriors] from around the world involved in local revolts and to direct them into an international battle seeking to create a single Islamist state. The organization began by mobilizing veterans from the war in Afghanistan already familiar with guerrilla fighting. Today, among other countries, al-Qa'ida is active in Afghanistan, Pakistan, Saudi Arabia, Yemen, the Sudan, Uzbekistan, Egypt, Syria, Lebanon, Jordan, the Palestinian territories, Algeria, Libya, Eritrea, Somalia, Bosnia, Chechnya, Indonesia, the Philippines, Malaysia, Germany, Britain, and the United States. Significantly, al-Qa'ida has crossed the Sunni-Shiite [religious] divide in that it also has contact with the Lebanese group, Hizballah.

AL-QA'IDA'S DIFFICULTIES AND ADVANTAGES

Al-Qa'ida's status as a non-state-sponsored terrorist organization creates both operational difficulties in the areas of financial and tactical operations and advantages in their choice of targets and missions. Without direct state aid, al-

Qa'ida raises money through three main sources: bin Ladin's own wealth and businesses; donations from mosques, schools, and charities; and collection of protection money. In the early 1990s, bin Ladin established several construction and farming businesses in Khartoum [Sudan] that provide income for al-Qa'ida, as well as a cover to attain weapons and to conceal operatives. Yet, without state funding, al-Qa'ida is susceptible to potential money problems; a freezing of private businesses' assets; and direct military attacks from states.

In addition to these considerations, al-Qa'ida misses out on several tactical benefits of state sponsorship such as intelligence, international documents, communications equipment, weapons, and specialized field training. This lack of specialized training makes the al-Qa'ida group more susceptible to infiltration, capture, and failure. For example, with the proposed bombing of the U.S. embassy in Paris, plotters made basic mistakes such as buying all of the chemicals needed for the bomb at the same place. However, as the September 11 [2001] attacks [on the United States] demonstrate, not all cells are so unsophisticated.

The absence of state sponsorship has its benefits too, such as the organization's flexibility and mobility. As Bruce Hoffman, author of *Inside Terrorism*, argues, this lack of specialized training gives the organization "enormous replicating ability." In commenting on the planned embassy bombing in Paris, a French interior ministry official acknowledged that detecting the terrorists would have been very difficult if they were better trained since they are able to blend into Western societies. He explained, "These people are pulled from our midst. . . .They are almost impossible to detect. If they get a little more sophistication and training, we could all be in more trouble."

In planning and staging the September 11 attacks, al-Qa'ida's leadership showed remarkable intelligence and flexibility in using their enemies' assets and openness against them. Al-Qa'ida terrorists have taken advantage of the political asylum system to gain a safe haven where they can raise money and create operational cells. Militants understood how to enter Western countries to the extent that more than half of the September 11 perpetrators passed through Britain before exploiting the disarray surrounding the U.S. visa system. Furthermore, with ample funding, they took advantage of U.S. educational opportunities, learned to fly airplanes in professional schools, and lived American lifestyles in normal American communities, and communicated with each other through coded Internet messages.

TRANSCENDING NATIONAL AND ETHNIC BOUNDARIES

Another benefit to not being sponsored by a state is that al-Qa'ida does not have a permanent central command center, which makes direct attacks on the organization more difficult. Organizational mobility also makes the group less vulnerable to being turned over to outside authorities. Perhaps most beneficial, non-affiliation with a state avoids any implication that the group is mercenary and makes its religious and communal bonds stronger. Cell members are tied to each other through a common belief and goal that transcend national and ethnic boundaries.

Yet al-Qa'ida's propaganda, training, and ideology give the group a reach beyond its own ranks. There is a misperception that bin Ladin and al-Qa'ida are tactically behind every terrorist attack connected to radical Islam. In reality, the role and tactics of al-Qa'ida are complicated since they are so multi-faceted. Al-Qa'ida adjusts its role to the situation by acting in a variety of manners that include training, funding, and organizing attacks. But both bin Ladin and al-Qa'ida also act consciously to encourage others to carry out operations on their own by providing inspiration and ideological justification.

One of bin Ladin's methods of supporting both his own and other forces launching attacks is the provision of training camps and guesthouses in Afghanistan, the Sudan, Yemen, and Pakistan for *mujahideen*. Within these camps, *mujahideen* are trained to forge travel documents, use covert communication techniques (such as encryption), and to handle and operate small arms and explosives. They are also indoctrinated to hate the West and to engage in jihad as they intensively study Islam and are shown videotapes to persuade them of the existence of a Western war against Muslims.

A SUPPORTIVE CONNECTION TO TERROR

Al-Qa'ida's ties to the 1993 World Trade Center bombing are an example of bin Ladin's connection to terror in this supportive capacity. Investigators believed that Ramzi Ahmed Yousef received financial support from bin Ladin and was sheltered in an al-Qa'ida guesthouse in Pakistan prior to his arrest. In addition, Ahmad Ajaj, who was convicted of the bombing, was in possession of an al-Qa'ida manual that included information on how to make bombs, conduct psychological warfare, and recruit new members. As far as actually planning the attack though, bin Ladin did not appear to be directly involved. The organization's role was one of support.

This is not a rare situation. For example, in 1999, Khalfan Khamis Mohamed, one of the Tanzania embassy bombers [who struck in 1998], told FBI agents that he had never met bin Ladin, heard him speak, or was even sure what he looked like. Individual cells seem to have a great deal of autonomy in choosing their targets and organizing their planning. Operatives are taught not only how to choose and destroy targets but also how to dress, behave, and support themselves financially. For example, Ahmad Ressam, the Algerian who was caught crossing the U.S.-Canadian border to stage attacks, told authorities that he was supposed to support himself through bank robberies and to select his own target.

By giving religious sanction for attacks, al-Qa'ida seeks to spread jihad beyond its own ranks. Though bin Ladin, as a non-cleric, has no authority to issue a *fatwa*, he authorizes killing for God's cause, offering the reward of paradise. In a 1998 interview with *Time*, bin Ladin stated, "Our job is to instigate, and by the grace of God, we did that." An example of this tactic is the 1995 car-bombing incident in Riyadh [Saudi Arabia]. Before their execution, four perpetrators of the bombing cited the influence of bin Ladin's communiques (in a forced confession) lending some credence to the theory that bin Ladin may not tactically have planned the attack, but did influence the action through his words.

INDIRECT AND DIRECT ACTION

In the same interview with *Time*, bin Ladin explained that the United States needed to realize that "thousands of millions of Muslims are angry" and would respond with a proportionate reaction. Bin Ladin's perceived ability to sanction killing and to inspire action coupled with the financial means to communicate his message are the factors that make him so dangerous. The danger that he represents is only further compounded by his popularity in the Arab and Muslim world for standing up to America and corrupt Arab regimes. Bin Ladin justifies actions against such regimes, like the attempted assassination of Egyptian President Husni

Mubarak, as proper since they are aimed at destroying a tyrant who is an unbeliever. Bin Ladin explained that actions against such regimes not adhering to Sharia are praiseworthy. They are "directed at the tyrants and the aggressors and the enemies of Allah, the tyrants, the traitors who commit acts of treason against their own countries and their own faith and their own prophet and their own nation.". . .

In addition to supporting actions through finances, training, and religious sanction, al-Qa'ida is involved in the direct planning of some operations. Despite the presence of many amateur warriors, al-Qa'ida cells and militant Islamist terrorists in general, reflect an extraordinary amount of patience, planning, and intelligence in their successful operations such as the 1998 embassy bombings, the bombing of the USS *Cole*, and the September 11 attacks. The embassy bombings were planned years in advance and involved a scale model manufactured in an Afghan camp. The *Cole* bombers took advantage of a four-hour window of opportunity available every other month to attack the U.S. naval vessel. The details and planning involved with the September 11 attacks ranging from how the perpetrators entered the country, to their flight training, to their surveillance of airport security, to their coordination of flights, are all remarkable.

Part of this detailed planning can be attributed to the Islamist militants' goal of an Islamic state ruled by Sharia coupled with their concept of the lengthy time it will take to reach such a goal. Bin Ladin and al-Qa'ida do not expect immediate results. They plan to wage their struggle over generations. Al-Qa'ida's concept of time gives it an advantage over counter-terror efforts. The United States and its allies perceive the terror problem as averting disaster today and tomorrow. Al-Qa'ida's ideology looks at developments and actions within the timeframe of a battle that will only end once the other side is defeated, and where all of their own casualties receive the ultimate reward of paradise. When law enforcement officials avert an attack, it is only a slight setback for al-Qa'ida. The organization only needs to be successful a small percentage of the time to achieve the effect they seek.

Something that might change this timeframe, though, is al-Qa'ida's attempt since 1993 to acquire weapons of mass destruction, according to the Federal Grand Jury indictment of bin Ladin. Bin Ladin called the acquisition of such weapons the "carrying out of a duty." The group contacted

Iraqi agents, among others, in an attempt to get a ready-made nuclear device as well as the materials and technology to construct their own nuclear weapon. The U.S. government thought that bin Ladin was a major investor in the al-Shifa pharmaceutical factory in Khartoum that was bombed by the United States in 1998 following the east Africa embassy bombings. The plant was believed to be an al-Qa'ida production site for a key component of VX nerve gas. The U.S. government believes that al-Qa'ida might try to create "dirty nukes," conventional weapons encased in radioactive substance that when exploded kill people by radiation poisoning.

AL-QA'IDA'S AMBIGUOUS RESUME

Because of the multi-faceted tactics of al-Qa'ida, U.S. officials seem to have difficulty pinning down bin Ladin's exact involvement in the anti-U.S. terror incidents of the last decade. Likewise, while bin Ladin is quick to commend terrorist acts against the United States, he avoids taking responsibility. For instance, in the case of the 1995 Riyadh car bombing that killed five Americans, bin Ladin praised the act, but denied involvement. While he has not taken outright responsibility for the September 11 attacks, bin Ladin provided religious justification for them indirectly through quoting the founder of Islam: "The destruction of the earth is more tolerable to God than killing a believer without cause." Bin Ladin applies this statement as God favoring destruction of the earth instead of the western infidel killing Muslims.

Other examples of praise, but not claim, are drawn from the Khobar bombing [in Al-Khobar, Saudi Arabia, in 1996] and a plan to assassinate [U.S.] President [Bill] Clinton in Manila. Bin Ladin referred to the Khobar bombing as a "great act in which I missed the honor of participating." As for his connection to Wali Khan, arrested for his plan to assassinate President Clinton, bin Ladin refused to comment on whether Khan worked for him. Yet he did say, "We are all together in this; we all work for Allah." Bin Ladin's reticence could be explained by his belief that his target audience, God, knows who committed the actions while other audiences are unimportant.

However, there are several incidents for which bin Ladin has either claimed responsibility or that were credibly linked to al-Qa'ida, such as the attempt to kill U.S. soldiers in route to Somalia in December 1992. Also in Somalia, al-Qa'ida took credit for providing training and help to Somalis that attacked U.S. soldiers and killed eighteen in Mogadishu at the beginning of October 1993. Al-Qa'ida is also linked to the previously mentioned 1995 assassination attempt of Egyptian president Mubarak and the 1995 bombing of the Egyptian embassy in Pakistan that was conducted by Egyptian Islamic Jihad. Until September 11, 2001, the most prominent al-Qa'ida attack was the August 1998 embassy bombings in Kenya and Tanzania that killed more than 250 people and injured more than 5500. The bombings occurred on the eighth anniversary of the United Nations' sanctions on Iraq. The main evidence linking bin Ladin to the attacks are an intercepted mobile phone conversation between two of bin Ladin's deputies and the testimony of Ali Mohamed, a former bin Ladin aide.

It seems as if al-Qa'ida attempted several missions to usher in the 2000 New Year as well. In December 1999, eleven Jordanians and two others trained in explosives in an al-Qa'ida camp were arrested in Amman for planning terrorist attacks on Christian tourist sites. In Kuwait, a man with ties to al-Qa'ida was arrested for planning to bomb American and Kuwaiti targets. The Kuwaiti police eventually uncovered that he was in possession of 300 pounds of explosives and a large number of detonators.

THE WEST'S PROBLEM WITH BIN LADIN AND AL-QA'IDA

The United States and the international media have helped to transform bin Ladin into something of a myth, a hero and popular man in the Islamic and Arab World. Yet despite some direct involvements, many of the ties between bin Ladin and the militant Islamist terror of the 1990s were indirect. To some extent, bin Ladin is the figurehead for the ideology of militant Islamism rather than "the spider at the center of a worldwide web plotting to attack American interests."

Still, after putting all myths aside, the threat that al-Qa'ida and bin Ladin pose is as real as the September 11 attacks. If bin Ladin was arrested or killed, al-Qa'ida would certainly feel the effects of the loss of his leadership, his financial backing, and his cult of personality. Yet the West's problem with al-Qa'ida, its distinct terrorist groups, and its cells would not disappear entirely. Al-Qa'ida supports these allied groups but does not control them. Each has its own distinct agenda that fits into al-Qa'ida's grander view of an Islamic struggle against the United States and its influences and would continue the struggle without bin Ladin. Bin Ladin designated Muhammad Atef, who has apparently predeceased him, as his successor. It is part of bin Ladin's doctrine to make plans for after his death, as martyrdom is a critical goal and he has expressed his willingness to die, be it sincere or otherwise. For this same reason, operations would not stop because of his absence, whether the group was led by al-Zawahiri or another leader.

The deep challenge that bin Ladin and al-Qa'ida represent is not just that of one man and an umbrella organization. Rather, it is the threat of a radical ideology that has grown more violent and more extreme with time and that has no interest in negotiation with the West. [*New York Times* journalist] Judith Miller states that between "50,000 and 70,000 militants from 55 different countries have trained in Afghanistan in recent years." Such a number of trained, armed, and angry warriors pose a big problem for the United States and its European, Arab, and Israeli allies, as long as there are Islamic leaders that not only give sanction, but proclaim it the duty of these warriors to commit jihad.

By the same token, though, the destruction of bin Ladin, his immediate lieutenants and network, and his Taliban hosts would be a major setback for the movement. Not only would this loss weaken the militants' ability to plan and carry out operations, but it would also undermine the myth that bin Ladin is the proper leader, his strategy the best strategy, and his doctrine the right doctrine.

Operations in Sudan

Michael Scheuer

After the Soviet-Afghan war, Osama bin Laden briefly
returned to Saudi Arabia. Then in 1991, the Saudis
exiled Bin Laden for carrying on his "holy war"
against America. He relocated to Sudan where he
continued to build his al Qaeda network, which began to carry out guerrilla and terrorist acts in various
nations. Al Qaeda's first major effort was to attack the
1992 U.S.-led famine relief effort in Somalia. Some of
Bin Laden's activities during his Sudan years, as well
as his 1992 return to Afghanistan, are related in this
excerpt from *Through Our Enemies' Eyes*. Although
this book was published anonymously, in 2004 its author was revealed to be Michael Scheuer, a CIA veteran who served as chief of the Bin Laden Unit at the
Counterterrorist Center from 1996 to 1999.

In late 1993 journalist Robert Fisk interviewed Osama bin
Laden while bin Laden was directing the construction of the
Khartoum-to-Port Sudan highway. One question Fisk asked
bin Laden was if he was running military training camps in
Sudan. Bin Laden indignantly answered Fisk, telling him the
idea was "the rubbish of the media and the embassies. I am
a construction engineer and an agriculturist. If I had training camps, I couldn't possibly do this job." Bin Laden was
not candid.

Between 1992 and bin Laden's return to Afghanistan, bin
Laden, [his two top military commanders] Abu Hafs al-Masri,
Abu Ubaydah, and their subordinates were, in essence, continuing to build and expand a self-supporting international
insurgent organization with which to attack U.S., Israeli,
Christian (almost exclusively Catholic), Egyptian, and other
pro-Western Muslim targets. As is known, however, bin
Laden did not publicly declare jihad on the United States until his 1996 return to Afghanistan. . . .

AL QAEDA'S TWO-STAGE PLAN

When the UN announced in late 1992 that it would put a U.S.-led multinational force in Somalia [the famine relief mission "Operation Restore Hope"], bin Laden quickly moved to damage U.S. units therein. His motivation was two-fold. First, after the USSR's demise, the United States became bin Laden's top enemy, and so U.S. troops were a natural target; bin Laden has said that after the UN stated its plans "the Muslim fighters headed for Somalia and another long battle, thinking that the Americans were like the Russians." The second motivation was a shared belief among bin Laden, his lieutenants, and senior National Islamic Front (NIF) leaders that "the United States would use Somalia as a staging ground to attack Sudan." In 1997, for example, bin Laden told the daily *Pakistan* that during the UN intervention, "the U.S. tried to make a base under the UN umbrella so that it could capture Sudan and Yemen."

Bin Laden believes the UN is Washington's tool and that even in 1992 the United States—as the UN readied for Somalia—was using it to force a "broad-based" government on the Afghans that would deny them and Islam the fruits of victory. Al Qaeda's quickly formulated plan for Somalia had two stages: interdicting U.S. forces traveling to Somalia, and attacking the forces after they arrived. In both cases, al Qaeda would use Arab Afghans and local Islamists. Two Yemeni comrades of bin Laden's, Jamal al-Hindi and Tariq al-Fahdli—the latter fought with bin Laden at Jalalabad [Afghanistan] in 1989 and was wounded—led a hastily improvised attack in Aden [Somalia], while bin Laden's top military leaders, Abu Ubaydah and Abu Hafs al-Masri, were charged with running al Qaeda's anti-U.S. operations in Somalia. Although a bit tabloidish, John Miller was on the mark when he wrote in *Esquire* that "when the Marines landed [in Somalia] in the last days of 1992, bin Laden sent in his own soldiers, armed with AK-47s and rocket launchers. Soon, using the techniques they had perfected against the Russians, they were shooting down American helicopters." Concurring, bin Laden has said, "the only non-Somali group that fought the Americans was the Arab Mujahedin brothers who had come from Afghanistan. . . . These were successful battles in which we inflicted big losses on the Americans. We used to hunt them down in Mogadishu [the capital of Somalia]."

HASTY ATTACKS

In Yemen, al Qaeda's attacks smacked of poor intelligence on the target and a lack of urban warfare skills. As UN forces assembled for Somalia, some U.S. military personnel transited Aden and occupied hotels for a few days. Al Qaeda focused on two hotels it believed the Americans used—the Gold Mohur and the Movenpick—and on 29 December 1992 detonated a bomb in the former. The bomb intended for the latter exploded prematurely in the hotel's parking lot. Overall, two tourists were killed and seven other people were wounded. Yemeni security arrested several men and found weapons and explosives in their truck in the Movenpick's parking lot. Although no U.S. soldiers were in the hotels when the attacks occurred—a nearby hotel did billet U.S. soldiers—they have entered al Qaeda battle lore as total victories, because within days after the attacks, all U.S. soldiers left Yemen.

In 1998 bin Laden summarized the standard version of the event. "The United States wanted to set up a military base for U.S. soldiers in Yemen so that it could send fresh troops to Somalia," bin Laden told the daily *Pakistan*. "The Arab mujahedin related to the Afghan jihad carried out two bomb explosions in Yemen to warn the United States, causing damage to some Americans staying in those hotels. The United States received our warning and gave up the idea of setting up its military bases in Yemen. This was the first al Qaeda victory scored against the Crusaders."

Interestingly, the al Qaeda attacks on U.S. targets in Aden occurred when the Yemeni regime was trying to stop a series of bombing and assassinations by Islamists in several areas of the country. The results of the Yemenis' investigation of the attempted hotel bombings and the other violent incidents pointed directly at bin Laden and [Ayman al-] Zawahiri's Egyptian Islamic Jihad (EIJ). Even before the hotel attacks, for example, the Yemenis had detained twenty individuals who claimed to be from the "Osama Group" and the "Islamic Jihad Organization." Although most Western terrorism experts identified the Yemeni Islamic Jihad, not bin Laden or Zawahiri, as the culprit for the hotel attacks, media reporting at the time—when put in the context of what since has been reported about bin Laden—strongly suggests the accuracy of his claim of responsibility. . . .

In Africa, bin Laden sent Abu Hafs al-Masri to Somalia to assess the prospects of success for the Arab Afghans he was deploying and to evaluate the ability of local Muslim tribesmen to absorb military training. On his return, Abu Hafs apparently reported positively and the future Nairobi embassy bombers Mohammed Sadiq Odeh, Mohammed Sadiq Howaida, and Fazul Abdullah Mohammed were among those sent to Mogadishu to train fighters from [Somali warlord] Farah Aideed's group. In total, bin Laden has said he sent 250 fighters to help Aideed and other Somali leaders fighting U.S.-led forces. The *Washington Post* has reported that after his capture in August 1998, Odeh told police "that he helped to train Islamic militants in Somalia who opposed the UN peacekeeping mission there." Islamabad's [Pakistan] the *News* said another alleged Nairobi bomber, Mohammed Sadiq Howaida, told Pakistani police after his August 1998 arrest that he was one of "a select group of Arabs" sent in 1993 to help Aideed, and [Arabic newspaper] *Al-Hayah* has reported Abu Ubaydah himself commanded just such a group "in the fight against U.S. forces in Somalia." In addition, journalist Mark Bowden in his brilliant book *Black Hawk Down* says, "Aideed's men received some expert guidance [on the use of rocket-propelled grenades] from Islamic soldiers smuggled in from Sudan, who had experience fighting Russian helicopters in Afghanistan. . . . Their fundamentalist advisers told them that the helicopter's tail rotor was its most vulnerable spot. So they learned to wait until it passed over, and to shoot up at it from behind." Bowden and others who have looked at the loss of two U.S. Black Hawk helicopters on 3 October 1993 report they were hit in the tail rotor by a rocket-propelled grenade.

POSITIVE RESULTS FOR AL QAEDA

While it is not yet possible to definitively document the military activities and successes of al Qaeda and its Somali trainees, al Qaeda fighters Howaida and Ali Muhammed—both now in jail in the United States—have said bin Laden's forces were directly involved in downing a U.S. helicopter and in two attacks using land mines. In 1997 bin Laden told Pakistani journalist Hamid Mirthat his fighters caught a helicopter pilot and "tied his legs, and dragged him through the streets," and when ABC correspondent John Miller interviewed bin Laden in May 1998, an unnamed bin Laden fighter told Miller "with a big grin" that he claimed credit for "slitting the throats of three American soldiers in Somalia."

Whether these attacks were made by al Qaeda fighters, local al Qaeda-trained Somali tribals, or a combination of both—which seems likely, because Abu Ubaydah led combat missions against U.S. forces in Somalia—is of little consequence in terms of the extremely positive impact they had on bin Laden's organization, its allies, and its international reputation. Bin Laden told *Al-Quds Al-Arabi*, "U.S. soldiers showed their cowardice and feebleness during the Somali experiment," and has since cited the attack in rhetorically challenging the U.S. military to come after him. "The Americans are cowards," bin Laden said in August 1997, "and cannot confront me. If they even think of confronting me, I will teach them a lesson similar to the lesson they were taught a few years ago in Somalia."

CASUALTIES OF GUERRILLA WAR

In addition to high-profile attacks in Yemen and Somalia, [during] . . . the 1992–1996 period . . . bin Laden was involved in other facets of the worldwide anti-U.S. insurgency he is conducting and striving to incite others to join. . . .

As in all wars, both sides took casualties. Bin Laden, his allies, and his associates were no exception in the 1992–1996 period. In February 1994, Pakistan captured [1993 World Trade Center bombing suspect] Ramzi Yousef and returned him to the United States; later in 1994, the Malaysians likewise caught and returned [al Qaeda member] Wali Khan Amin Shah. In late 1994, Gama'at al-Islamiyya (IG) leader Anwar Shaban was ambushed and killed by security forces in Bosnia, and many Arab Afghans evacuated Bosnia after the Dayton Accord [which ended the Bosnian war in 1995].

In addition, [Arabic newspaper] *Al-Sharq Al-Awsat* has reported that the Bosnian war cost bin Laden's allies a large loss of veteran fighters. Captured EIJ fighters have told Egyptian courts that in Bosnia "a large number of the Organization's [EIJ's] members" were uncovered. "Bosnia was an open field for the arrest of many Jihad and Islamic Group members when they tried to turn Bosnia into another Afghanistan in the heart of Europe and to move the phenomenon of Afghan Arabs to it." Attacks on the pope, President Clinton, and U.S. airlines were halted, and the [1995] attack on [Egyptian president Hosni] Mubarak in Addis Ababa [Egypt] was unsuccessful and almost all of the attackers were killed or captured. Egyptian security forces also stopped a second planned attack on Mubarak in Cairo [Egypt] in December 1995. Likewise, most of the team that executed the November 1995 attack on Egypt's embassy in Islamabad were killed or captured. Another senior Europe-based IG leader, Talat Fuad Kassem, disappeared while transiting Croatia in September 1995. It was later reported that bin Laden valued Kassem as highly as he has EIJ leader Zawahiri.

Wins and losses, triumphs and disasters, these are the characteristics of all wars. But in a guerrilla war, as has been seen in Afghanistan, Kashmir [territory divided among Pakistan, India, and China], Vietnam, and elsewhere, if the guerrilla force survives, it is winning. And bin Laden's organization not only survived this four-year period, but also grew in size, reach, and capability; made new friends and allies; learned how to plan for, absorb, and survive the losses of war; and relocated to Afghanistan, an area more remote and less vulnerable than Sudan.

SUDAN HEATS UP

After he had spent five productive years in Sudan, several factors coalesced to cause bin Laden to go to Afghanistan for the third time since 1979. In the first instance, Sudan had heated up markedly in terms of earning the West's attention and enmity since bin Laden arrived in 1992. The NIF's open-door for Arabs—Arabs coming to Sudan in the bin Laden years needed no visas—made Khartoum [Sudan] a haven for Islamist insurgents and terrorists. By the middle of bin Laden's stay, the EIJ; the IG; HAMAS (Islamic Resistance Movement); the Palestine Islamic Jihad; the ANO [Abu Nidal Organization]; several Algerian, Libyan, and Tunisian groups; the Eritrean Islamic Jihad; groups of Ethiopian, Uganda, and Somali Islamists; and Lebanese Hizballah—among others—were in Khartoum. The combination of hosting these Islamist fighters and bin Laden's presence, at least after it was clear he aided the attacks on Mubarak and OPM-SANG [U.S. Office of Program Management–Saudi Arabian National Guard, bombed in 1995], led the United States to name Sudan a state sponsor of terrorism, an act followed by the imposition of U.S. and UN sanctions. These sanctions were one more strain on NIF leader [Hasan al-] Turabi's fledgling Islamic state, which already was fighting a protracted civil war with Sudanese Christians; fencing with Egypt over the attack on Mubarak, boundary demarcation, and access to Nile waters; suffering from a decaying economy; and being loudly criticized by the international community for abusing human rights and limiting freedom of worship. By early 1996, then, Sudan was becoming too hot for bin Laden, and bin Laden was another point of irritation between the West and Sudan that Turabi did not need.

A Target for Assassination

Two other factors also motivated bin Laden to leave Sudan. First, he was again a target for assassination; two attacks failed in early 1994. On 4 February Takfir al-Hijra fighters— a group that thinks bin Laden is not a strict enough Muslim —tried to kill bin Laden in the meeting hall next to his Khartoum home. The attack was defeated by bin Laden's bodyguard and Sudanese security. In the battle bin Laden and his eldest son Abdallah returned fire with AK-47s. "We used to meet [at my residence compound] with the brother guests at 1700 hours every evening," bin Laden told [Arabic newspaper] *Al-Quds Al-Arabi* in 1996.

> On that day, and for a reason known to God, I was late. Then I heard a barrage of bullets fired on the guest [meeting?] room, which is detached from the house. Some bullets were [fired] at me. So I took my weapon and went to a position overlooking the house to investigate the matter. I gave my eldest son (Abdallah) a weapon and told him to take a position inside the house. I thought that an armed group had attacked the guards, and we prepared ourselves for a clash. But it was discovered that the attack was aimed directly at the guest room, which was stormed by three young men who opened fire at the guests, three of whom were seriously wounded. They opened fire on the place where I use to sit. One [guest] was hit in the abdomen, another in the thigh, and the third in the leg. The brothers clashed with them. There were Sudanese security forces near the house, so they clashed with them, killing two and wounding the third. Some of the brothers sustained minor injuries.

A few weeks later, the Takfir attacked and killed worshipers at Friday prayers in the Al-Thawrah Mosque in the Omdurman section of Khartoum where bin Laden may have been present. Bin Laden says he was there during the attack, but media reports say he was not and that his absence may have saved his life.

Pressure from the Saudis

The final factor prompting bin Laden's departure from Sudan was the increasing discomfort of the Saudi regime and the al-Saud family with bin Laden's public criticism and defiance of them; Riyadh [capital of Saudi Arabia], along with the Qataris [citizens of Qatar], had been a major benefactor of the Sudanese NIF even before it took power and did not look kindly on the NIF hosting bin Laden. After bin Laden left the kingdom in April 1991, Saudi authorities continued to act against him. In late 1991, for example, Riyadh revoked the passport he traveled on to Pakistan, announcing that Saudi intelligence had found that bin Laden was smuggling weapons to Yemen from the kingdom. Then, at some point in 1992, according to the Associated Press, "Saudi Arabia froze his [bin Laden's] bank accounts" in the kingdom.

In addition, Mary Anne Weaver has reported in the *Atlantic Monthly* that the Saudis sent "hit teams" to Sudan in the 1991–1992 period to kill bin Laden, a point supported by the testimony in a U.S. court of an al Qaeda defector who was close to bin Laden in Sudan. On 16 May 1993 Riyadh issued an arrest warrant for bin Laden "both because of his support for fundamentalist groups involved in terrorist operations in Algeria and Egypt and because of his ties with upstart religious circles [read: religious critics of the al-Sauds] that tried to establish an independent human rights organization in Saudi Arabia at the beginning of May [1993]." Given the usual glacierlike movement of Saudi bureaucrats, the speed with which the warrant was issued after the start of the human rights campaign—no more than sixteen days— —it is reasonable to assume the warrant was issued because of the latter, not the former.

SEEKING AN ALTERNATIVE LAND

By late 1994, ensuring that bin Laden did not reenter the kingdom was not sufficient for Saudi authorities. In September, Saudi security forces arrested some of the harshest religious critics of the al-Sauds. Included were Shaykh al-Awdah and Shaykh al-Hawali, two clerics whom bin Laden has long identified as his personal heroes and the rightful leaders of Islam's jihad against America. When the clerics were arrested and "the State prevented the clerics from speaking," bin Laden has said he and his colleagues in Sudan "set up the advice committee [the London-based Advice and Reform Committee (ARC)] and began to reveal the truth and clarify matters [to the Saudi people], seeking reform and guidance for the nation, and reminding people of the long time our Ulema had spent working to reform [Saudi society] through good preaching." Bin Laden told Abd al-Bari Atwan of *Al-Quds Al-Arabi* that ARC communiqués, issued from Sudan and London, were ready by the Saudi people, and

> when the Saudi government discovered the great impact and effect of these statements, it transcended all its disagreements with the Sudanese regime, which had exerted great efforts to rectify its relations with the Riyadh government and to end the [Saudi] boycott [against Khartoum] but encountered a lack of response and arrogance [from Riyadh]. After [ARC] Statement No. 17—it was an open letter to the King on the occasion of the cabinet reshuffle—the Saudi Government contracted the Sudanese Government at the highest level, requesting [Saudi-Sudanese] reconciliation on the condition that Osama bin Laden and the sons of the two Holy Mosques accompanying him in Sudan were expelled and that they stopped [sic] issuing statements. The Sudanese Government at the highest level informed me of its difficult position and the scale of Saudi pressure. They [the Sudanese] asked me to stop issuing statements. On the day I was told to stop issuing statements I sought to find an alternative land capable of bearing the word of truth and we came to the land of Khorasan [Afghanistan] once again.

THE SAUDIS SEND AN OLIVE BRANCH

While pressing the NIF to oust bin Laden, the Saudis simultaneously sent olive-branch-carrying envoys to Sudan to try to get bin Laden to reconcile with the al-Sauds and return home. These emissaries, bin Laden said, told him he could return to Saudi Arabia and receive "my identity card, passport, and money . . . if I say through the media that the King is a good Muslim." "I would like to state," bin Laden told ABC in late 1998, "that the Saudi government initiated contacts [with me] during the last period in Sudan. They sent several delegations to enter into negotiations aimed at convincing me to keep silent on the unjust American occupation of the land of the two mosques." Among the envoys were bin Laden's mother and Bakr bin Laden, his eldest brother and family patriarch; bin Laden told Robert Fisk the al-Sauds "had offered his family 2 billion riyals ($535 million) if he abandons his 'holy war'"—a tactic like the al-Sauds' earlier offer of a $90 million construction contract to deflect bin Laden's focus from the Afghan jihad. As an unnamed acquaintance of bin Laden has said, "He is so kind and tender toward his kinsmen. But this has nothing to do with the formulation of his platform or decisions."

Bin Laden turned the emissaries down flat, thereby precipitating another Saudi move against him. Having issued an arrest warrant, Riyadh was now faced with the terrifying possibility that at some point someone would seize and return an unrepentant bin Laden to the kingdom, thereby making him a rallying point for internal dissidents. Cornered by a dilemma of their own making, the Saudis moved on 10 April 1994 to erase the problem by withdrawing bin Laden's nationality, a sort of a de-Saudification process. Officially, the interior ministry's decree said bin Laden's nationality was canceled because he engaged in "irresponsible acts which run counter to the Kingdom's interest and offend against its relations with sister countries, and for his failure to comply with instructions." In traditional Saudi head-in-the-sand fashion, Riyadh tried to frame the bin Laden issue—he had not yet staged an attack in the kingdom—as the world's problem, not its own. After the November 1995 bombing of the OPM-SANG building, the Saudis moved to further refine this portrait to make it appear the confrontation was exclusively between bin Laden and the United States.

DEPARTURE FOR AFGHANISTAN

With pressures converging, bin Laden decided to leave Sudan by early May 1996. At the time, bin Laden was silent about his departure and by his silence allowed the NIF to appear responsive to Saudi concerns and, partially, to U.S. and UN demands that Sudan stop supporting terrorism. The NIF did not claim that it deported bin Laden, but it did nothing at first to negate that impression. It appears that its silence on this score angered some pro-bin Laden NIF members in Sudan and abroad, a lesson the Taliban regime surely has taken to heart. In early 1997, for example, Sudan's information ministry said Sudan did not deport bin Laden and "the Afghan brothers" and that "Sheikh Osama and the Afghan brothers left Sudan of their own volition, knowing the pressures Sudan is facing and so that they can destroy the opportunity for the enemies of Islam and Sudan." Later, in April 1997, NIF leader Turabi underscored that bin Laden decided to leave because he saw his presence "was at the root of much pressure exercised by Saudi Arabi and the United States on the government in Khartoum."

The Arab media pretty much agreed with official Sudanese commentary, with [the Sudanese city of] Amman's [newspaper] *Sawt al-Mar'ah* saying that bin Laden left "voluntarily . . .

[and] his departure from Khartoum had nothing to do with Washington's demands," and *Al-Watan Al-Arabi* simply asserting that bin Laden decided to leave Sudan "to reduce regional and international pressure on Turabi and to prevent further sanctions on Sudan." Long after his departure, bin Laden in May 1998 said he left the country because he "felt the government of Sudan could not afford to bear [U.S.] pressure any more."

On balance, I believe bin Laden decided to leave Sudan on his own hook because of the assassination attempts, because he saw a need to ease international pressure on Turabi's new Islamic state, and because he had decided it was time to intensify his anti-U.S. guerrilla war from a redoubt that offered tremendous topographical advantages to the defender.

Why We Fight the Infidels

Al Qaeda

While investigating Osama bin Laden in 2000, the U.S. Federal Bureau of Investigation made a remarkable find. A raid of an al Qaeda guest house in Manchester, England, produced the al Qaeda training manual, entitled "Military Studies in the Jihad Against the Tyrants." The manual offers al Qaeda members detailed instructions in many guerrilla activities, including forging documents, buying and transporting weapons, communicating with other members, and carrying out assassinations. Whether or not Osama bin Laden actually wrote this 180-page document, it undoubtedly reflects his thinking and possibly received his approval. The introductory comments excerpted here reveal al Qaeda's historical justification for its struggle, as well as its determination to achieve its goals by violent rather than peaceful means.

PLEDGE, O SISTER

To the sister believer whose clothes the criminals have stripped off.

To the sister believer whose hair the oppressors have shaved.

To the sister believer [whose] body has been abused by the human dogs. . . .

Pledge, O Sister

Covenant, O Sister . . . to make their women widows and their children orphans.

Covenant, O Sister . . . to make them desire death and hate appointments and prestige.

Covenant, O Sister . . . to slaughter them like lambs and let the Nile, al-Asi, and Euphrates rivers flow with their blood.

Al Qaeda, "Military Studies in the Jihad Against the Tyrants," translated by the United States Department of Justice, www.usdoj.gov.

Covenant, O Sister . . . to be a pick of destruction for every godless and apostate regime.

Covenant, O Sister . . . to retaliate for you against every dog who touch you even with a bad word.

A HOLY INVOCATION

In the name of Allah, the merciful and compassionate

Thanks be to Allah. We thank him, turn to him, ask his forgiveness, and seek refuge in him from our wicked souls and bad deeds. Whomever Allah enlightens will not be misguided, and the deceiver will never be guided. I declare that there is no god but Allah alone; he has no partners. I also declare that Mohammed is his servant and prophet.

[Koranic verses]:

"O ye who believe! Fear Allah as He should be feared, and die not except in a state of Islam"

"O mankind! Fear your guardian lord who created you from a single person. Created, out of it, his mate, and from them twain scattered [like seeds] countless men and women; fear Allah, through whom ye demand your mutual [rights], and be heedful of the wombs [that bore you]: for Allah ever watches over you."

"O ye who believe! Fear Allah, and make your utterance straight forward: That he may make your conduct whole and sound and forgive you your sins. He that obeys Allah and his messenger, has already attained the great victory."

Afterword,

The most truthful saying is the book of Allah and the best guidance is that of Mohammed, God bless and keep him. [Therefore,] the worst thing is to introduce something new, for every novelty is an act of heresy and each heresy is a deception.

FROM COLONIALISM TO APOSTASY

Martyrs were killed, women were widowed, children were orphaned, men were handcuffed, chaste women's heads were shaved, harlots' heads were crowned, atrocities were inflicted on the innocent, gifts were given to the wicked, virgins were raped on the prostitution alter . . .

After the fall of our orthodox caliphates [governments] on March 3, 1924 and after expelling the colonialists, our Islamic nation was afflicted with apostate rulers who took over in the Moslem nation. These rulers turned out to be more infidel and criminal than the colonialists themselves. Moslems have endured all kinds of harm, oppression, and torture at their hands.

Those apostate rulers threw thousands of the Haraka Al-Islamyia (Islamic Movement) youth in gloomy jails and detention centers that were equipped with the most modern

---

BLENDING IN AMONG THE ENEMY

Al Qaeda members have proven skillful at blending into Western surroundings without attracting attention. Some of the hijackers of September 11, 2001, for example, attended U.S. flight schools. The following excerpt from "Military Studies in the Jihad Against the Tyrants" justifies a Muslim altering his appearance and behavior in order to fight the enemy.

How can a Muslim spy live among enemies if he maintains his Islamic characteristics? How can he perform his duties to Allah and not want to appear Muslim?

Concerning the issue of clothing and appearance (appearance of true religion), [Islamic theologian] Ibn Taimia—may Allah have mercy on him—said, "If a Muslim is in a combat or godless area, he is not obligated to have a different appearance from [those around him]. The [Muslim] man may prefer or even be obligated to look like them, provided his action brings a religious benefit of preaching to them, learning their secrets and informing Muslims, preventing their harm, or some other beneficial goal."

Resembling the polytheist [i.e., non-Muslim] in religious appearance is a kind of "necessity permits the forbidden" even though they [forbidden acts] are basically prohibited. As for the visible duties, like fasting and praying, he can fast by using any justification not to eat with them [polytheist]. As for prayer, the book (Al-Manhaj Al-Haraki Lissira Al-Nabawiya) quotes [Islamic theologian] Al-Bakhari that "he [the Moslem] may combine the noon and afternoon [prayers], sunset and evening [prayers]. That is based on the fact that the prophet— Allah bless and keep him—combined [prayers] in Madina [the second holy city of Islam] without fear or hesitation."

Though scholars have disagreed about the interpretation of that tradition, it is possible—though Allah knows best—that the Moslem spy combines [prayers]. It is noted, however, that it is forbidden to do the unlawful, such as drinking wine or fornicating. There is nothing that permits those.

"Military Studies in the Jihad Against the Tyrants," United States Department of Justice. www.usdoj.gov:80/ag/trainingmanual.htm.

torture devices and [manned with] experts in oppression and torture. Those youth had refused to move in the rulers' orbit, obscure matters to the youth, and oppose the idea of rebelling against the rulers. But they [the rulers] did not stop there; they started to fragment the essence of the Islamic nation by trying to eradicate its Moslem identity. Thus, they started spreading godless and atheistic views among the youth. We found some that claimed that socialism was from Islam, democracy was the [religious] council, and the prophet— God bless and keep him—propagandized communism.

THE WILL OF THE RULERS

Colonialism and its followers, the apostate rulers, then started to openly erect crusader centers, societies, and organizations like Masonic Lodges, Lions and Rotary clubs, and foreign schools. They aimed at producing a wasted generation that pursued everything that is western and produced rulers, ministers, leaders, physicians, engineers, businessmen, politicians, journalists, and information specialists. [Koranic verse:] "And Allah's enemies plotted and planned, and Allah too planned, and the best of planners is Allah."

They [the rulers] tried, using every means and [kind of] seduction, to produce a generation of young men that did not know [anything] except what they [the rulers] want, did not say except what they [the rulers] think about, did not live except according to their [the rulers'] way, and did not dress except in their [the rulers'] clothes. However, majestic Allah turned their deception back on them, as a large group of those young men who were raised by them [the rulers] woke up from their sleep and returned to Allah, regretting and repenting.

The young men returning to Allah realized that Islam is not just performing rituals but a complete system: Religion and government, worship and Jihad [holy war], ethics and dealing with people, and the Koran and sword. The bitter situation that the nation has reached is a result of its divergence from Allah's course and his righteous law for all places and times. That [bitter situation] came about as a result of its children's love for the world, their loathing of death, and their abandonment of Jihad [holy war].

Unbelief is still the same. It pushed [Mohammed's opponent] Abou Jahl—may Allah curse him—and [Mohammed's opponent] Kureish's valiant infidels to battle the prophet—

God bless and keep him—and to torture his companions—
may Allah's grace be on them. It is the same unbelief that
drove [the late Egyptian president Anwar] Sadat, [the current
Egyptian president] Hosni Mubarak, [Libyan president
Muammar al] Gadhafi, [the late Syrian president] Hafez As-
sad, [Yemeni president Ali Abdullah] Saleh, [King] Fahed
[bin Abdul Aziz of Saudi Arabia]—Allah's curse be upon the
non-believing leaders—and all the apostate Arab rulers to
torture, kill, imprison, and torment Moslems.

No Truce or Diplomacy

These young men realized that an Islamic government
would never be established except by the bomb and rifle. Islam does not coincide or make a truce with unbelief, but
rather confronts it.

The confrontation that Islam calls for with these godless
and apostate regimes, does not know Socratic debates, Pla-
tonic ideals nor Aristotelian diplomacy. But it knows the dialogue of bullets, the ideals of assassination, bombing, and destruction, and the diplomacy of the cannon and machine-gun.

The young came to prepare themselves for Jihad [holy
war], commanded by the majestic Allah's order in the holy
Koran. [Koranic verse:] "Against them make ready your
strength to the utmost of your power, including steeds of
war, to strike terror into (the hearts of) the enemies of Allah
and your enemies, and others besides whom ye may not
know, but whom Allah doth know."

I present this humble effort to these young Moslem men
who are pure, believing, and fighting for the cause of Allah.
It is my contribution toward paving the road that leads to
majestic Allah and establishes a caliphate according to the
prophecy.

CHAPTER 3

BIN LADEN'S WAR AGAINST AMERICA

PEOPLE
WHO MADE
HISTORY

OSAMA BIN LADEN

Al Qaeda Bombs U.S. Embassies in Kenya and Tanzania

Simon Reeve

Osama bin Laden attracted little Western attention in February 1998 when he issued his second declaration of war against America. But on August 7 of that year, Bin Laden and al Qaeda achieved worldwide notoriety by successfully bombing two U.S. embassies in Tanzania and Kenya. Two hundred twenty-four people were killed in the attacks, most of them Africans; more than forty-five hundred people were injured. In the following excerpt from his book *The New Jackals*, investigative journalist Simon Reeve relates the planning and execution of the bombings, which took place within ten minutes of one another. Reeve also describes the ineffective U.S. military retaliation against al Qaeda and explains how the bombings enhanced Bin Laden's power and prestige. Reeve is also the author of *One Day in September: The Full Story of the 1972 Munich Olympics Massacre.*

After issuing his "declaration of war" against America in February 1998, there was little chance that Osama bin Laden would keep quiet for long. He might have been living in relative isolation in Afghanistan, under threat of abduction by American forces and under intense satellite scrutiny, but bin Laden needed to hit the Americans hard if he was to back up his threats with actions.

A GATHERING OF MILITANTS

Bin Laden decided to put his al Qaeda terrorist cell in east Africa into action. The cell had been established in 1994, when Mohamed Sadeek Odeh, a slender young militant Palestinian from Jordan, moved into a modest house in the city of

Simon Reeve, *The New Jackals: Ramzi Yousef, Osama bin Laden and the Future of Terrorism.* Boston: Northeastern University Press, 1999. Copyright © 1999 by University Press of New England, Hanover, NH. All rights reserved. Reproduced by permission.

Mombasa on the Kenyan coast. Odeh had received terrorist
training in Afghanistan before he joined al Qaeda in 1992, allegedly pledging allegiance to bin Laden at a camp in the
Hindu Kush mountains. His first assignment had been Somalia, where US intelligence sources claim he trained fighters
who killed 18 American soldiers. In Kenya he bought a seven-
tonne boat and set up a fishing business "with al Qaeda
money." Catches from the boat were used to support other al
Qaeda members who then began arriving in the country.

In the years that followed other bin Laden militants quietly settled in Kenya. Fazul Abdullah Mohammed, for example, had fallen under bin Laden's spell while he studied in
Khartoum [Sudan]. The young militant, originally from the
town of Moroni on the stunning island of Comoros in the In-
dian Ocean, arrived in Kenya with his wife Hamila and two
young children, and began living with and working for
Wadih El Hage, the senior al Qaeda man in the country. El
Hage had arrived in Kenya from Khartoum and taken command of the east Africa cell, renting a comfortable house on
the Fedha Estate near Nairobi airport for £300 a month
($500), opening businesses that would act as fronts for al
Qaeda, and pretending to work for a charity called Help
Africa People. His five children went to local schools and his
wife April even joined the local Parent-Teacher Association.

AWAITING THE CALL TO ARMS

It was an astonishing international operation paralleled by
the actions of other al Qaeda "sleeper" units in countries
such as Britain and America. These men spent years establishing themselves in an alien country, living perfectly re-
spectable lives, waiting for nothing more than a call to arms
from Osama bin Laden. Yet they were not completely in the
shadows. The FBI, CIA, MI6, and the intelligence services of
almost every country in the Middle East were either monitoring or investigating al Qaeda by 1996, and by 1997 American investigators knew al Qaeda was established in Kenya
and east Africa. Wadih El Hage was even questioned by the
FBI in New York on several occasions in September 1997,
and in Texas again in October of the same year: on all occasions he allegedly lied about his contacts with al Qaeda. The
CIA also had informants working within the east Africa cell,
but they apparently failed to warn of bin Laden's plans.

By the end of July 1998, the east Africa al Qaeda cell had

been turned into an operational terrorist unit ready to attack US embassies. Mohamed Rashed Daoud Al-'Owhali, an aspiring terrorist who had asked bin Laden for "a mission," arrived in Nairobi from Lahore, Pakistan, on 31 July, having filmed a videotape with a man called "Azzam" to "celebrate their anticipated 'martyrdom.'" The gang converged at 43 Rundu Estates, Nairobi, a two-storey unfurnished house and garage surrounded by a high wall and hedge, which Fazul Abdullah Mohammed had rented. They were not planning a long stay. The east African cell assembled in the house and began making their final preparations. The brother-in-law of their landlady was among those the gang would kill.

NEARLY SIMULTANEOUS BOMBINGS

By the evening of 6 August 1998, both the bomb and the gang were ready. Odeh, the senior terrorist, had been told to leave the city, and using an assumed name he flew out of Nairobi on Pakistani International Airways flight 746, heading towards Pakistan. Early the next morning Fazul Abdullah Mohammed climbed behind the wheel of a white pick up truck parked at the gang's villa. Carrying four stun grenades and a handgun, Al-'Owhali jumped into a larger Toyota truck driven by Azzam—a massive bomb sat in the back. Together the two vehicles wound their way through Nairobi's busy streets, and headed towards the American embassy in the city.

At 10.30 A.M. the battered bomb truck pulled up at the back of the embassy, and Al-'Owhali jumped out, lobbed a stun grenade in the direction of a Kenyan security guard, and turned and ran. Instead of immediately reaching for the detonator, Azzam fired his handgun at the windows of the embassy, giving Al-'Owhali precious seconds to round a corner. He escaped the worst of the massive blast that followed seconds later when Azzam detonated the bomb, blowing himself to pieces, demolishing a multi-storey secretarial college, and severely damaging the US embassy and the Co-operative Bank Building. At least 213 people died and more than 4,500 were injured.

Within 10 minutes of the Nairobi blast a second van bomb exploded outside the US embassy in Dar-es-Salaam in Tanzania, killing 11 people and injuring another 85. The blast was so powerful that the body of the suicide-bomber driving the van was cut in two, and the top half of his torso hit the embassy building still clutching the steering-wheel in both hands.

THE U.S. STRIKES AT AL QAEDA

*On August 20, 1998, the United States responded to the
embassy bombings in Kenya and Tanzania with retalia-
tory strikes against al Qaeda. President Bill Clinton broadcast
the following announcement from Edgartown Elementary
School in Martha's Vineyard, Massachusetts.*

Good afternoon. Today I ordered our Armed Forces to strike
at terrorist-related facilities in Afghanistan and Sudan because of the threat they present to our national security.

I have said many times that terrorism is one of the greatest
dangers we face in this new global era. We saw its twisted
mentality at work last week in the embassy bombings in
Nairobi and Dar es Salaam, which took the lives of innocent
Americans and Africans and injured thousands more. Today
we have struck back.

The United States launched an attack this morning on one
of the most active terrorist bases in the world. It is located in
Afghanistan and operated by groups affiliated with Osama
bin Laden, a network not sponsored by any state, but as dangerous as any we face. We also struck a chemical weapons-
related facility in Sudan. Our target was the terrorists' base of
operation and infrastructure. Our objective was to damage
their capacity to strike at Americans and other innocent
people.

I ordered this action for four reasons: First, because we
have convincing evidence these groups played the key role in
the embassy bombings in Kenya and Tanzania. Second, because these groups have executed terrorist attacks against
Americans in the past. Third, because we have compelling information that they were planning additional terrorist attacks
against our citizens and others with the inevitable collateral
casualties we saw so tragically in Africa. And, fourth, because
they are seeking to acquire chemical weapons and other dangerous weapons.

Terrorists must have no doubt that, in the face of their
threats, America will protect its citizens and will continue to
lead the world's fight for peace, freedom and security.

Now I am returning to Washington to be briefed by my National Security team on the latest information. I will provide
you with a more detailed statement later this afternoon from
the White House.

Thank you very much.

U.S. State Department, "President Clinton Announces Strikes," August 20, 1998.
http://usinfo.state.gov.

BIN LADEN IS THE IMMEDIATE SUSPECT

For the Kenyan police and scores of FBI agents who arrived within hours to investigate the bombing, Osama bin Laden was the immediate suspect. "He was top of a short list" of men capable of pulling off the double attacks, according to an American source familiar with the investigation. There was concern, however, at the depth of planning for the double attack. "Two at once is not twice as hard," said Milton Bearden, a retired senior CIA official who has served as the agency's ranking officer in Afghanistan, Pakistan and Sudan. "Two at once is a hundred times as hard."

The bombings showed that despite years of investigation and monitoring by the world's intelligence services, al Qaeda was still a powerful terrorist force worthy of a James Bond movie. American intelligence later realized al Qaeda had also been planning other attacks on American interests in Kampala, Uganda, to coincide with the bombings in east Africa, but they were delayed at the last moment, giving police the time to swoop and arrest 18 terrorists over the following two weeks. "The attacks were planned to be more serious and devastating than those in Nairobi and Dar-es-Salaam," Muruli Mukasa, the Ugandan State Minister for Security, said later.

Despite the sophistication of al Qaeda's attack, the escape plans of the terrorists left a lot to be desired. When Odeh fled to Pakistan, he took a direct flight and carried documents that did not even bear his photograph. He was arrested, interrogated by Pakistani intelligence agents, and later deported to the United States to face charges. "I did it all for the cause of Islam. [Osama bin Laden] is my leader, and I obey his orders," he allegedly said.

In Kenya Fazul Abdullah Mohammed escaped the immediate dragnet via the Comoros. Al-'Owhali, the would-be suicide bomber, survived the Nairobi blast and was taken to the MP Shah Hospital. Suspicious doctors noted that his injuries appeared to indicate he had been running away from the bomb when it exploded. When the FBI came calling a few days later the doctors mentioned the Arab patient, a taxi driver remembered taking him to an address in Nairobi from the hospital, and the police picked him up. Within days of the bombings the FBI had two strong suspects in custody, and were actively seeking their supporters and backers. Al-'Owhali broke down and gave crucial details. Other suspects were picked up across east Africa and the cell began to unravel.

THE FAILURE OF THE U.S. MILITARY RESPONSE

By the time President Clinton launched Tomahawk cruise missiles against bin Laden's base at Zhawar Kili, south-west of the Afghan town of Khost, his administration had accumulated a wealth of information on al Qaeda. The President's instructions were simple: take it down.

At CIA headquarters in Langley after the missile strikes, agents, analysts and senior officials crowded into the room used by the Counterterrorism Center for crisis management (nicknamed the "fusion centre"). Stuffed with phones, more than a dozen computers linked directly to giant mainframes in the basement, and large monitor screens displaying satellite photos and the latest media reports, the fusion centre has been witness to both hideous failure and spectacular success. A burn mark on the carpet marks the spot where George Tenet, the down-to-earth, burger-loving Director of the CIA [from 1997 to 2004], dropped his cigar in excitement at the news that Mir Aimal Kansi, who killed two CIA employees outside the Langley HQ, had been captured in Pakistan in June 1997.

Imagine the palpable sense of disappointment in the fusion centre when translators heard bin Laden talking in a radio message beamed out over Afghanistan and Pakistan after the missile strikes: "By the grace of Allah, I am alive!" he said.

Bin Laden had been warned that America was tracking him via his phone just hours before the attack, allegedly by supporters working for Pakistani intelligence, and he switched it off. "He turned the lights out," said one intelligence source. Bin Laden also cancelled a meeting at Zhawar Kili after discovering that 180 American diplomats were withdrawing from Islamabad [Pakistan] on a chartered plane. He correctly assumed it was to prevent retaliation after an imminent strike, and was actually hundreds of miles away in northern Afghanistan when the missiles landed.

The wisdom of the attacks on Sudan must also be questioned. The US government initially said simply that the Al Shifa pharmaceutical factory was connected with bin Laden and was producing chemicals used to manufacture chemical weapons. However, CIA agents involved in identifying the factory as a risk were not aware it was producing medicines for human and veterinary use until they checked the factory's Internet web-site after their missiles had ripped it to pieces. In the rubble reporters found packaging for the company's "Profenil" brand of ibuprofen, a common anti-inflammatory drug and pain reliever, and boxes of veterinary antibiotics plastered with pictures of goats, camels and sheep.

A HARD MAN TO KILL

If the missile strikes were designed as a surgical operation to crush al Qaeda, they failed. Most of the bases hit in Afghanistan had no connection with bin Laden. Among the survivors from those bases who were linked to bin Laden, support for him was redoubled. Mohammad Hussain, an 18-year-old militant training in the camps when the bombs fell, was left with deep wounds in his back and chest. Six of his friends were killed. "I could smell perfume from the blood of those martyrs," he said. "We will take revenge from America and its president. They should not think we are weak. We will emerge as heroes of Islam like Osama bin Laden."

Bin Laden would never be an easy man to kill; he is no fool. Consider the experience of Peter Jouvenal, a British cameraman who went to interview him. "We were called at our hotel and left in the middle of the night," said Jouvenal. "We were blindfolded and the car stopped on a mountain road. There we were body-searched and a metal detector was passed over us, three times. We were told to confess if we had any tracking devices. When we met [bin Laden] I was not allowed to use my own camera. They had their own one, which worked. They're not stupid. They know all about modern technology and they know what they're doing."

Optimistic Westerners who dismiss bin Laden as a paper tiger should consider the wars he has already fought and study his words. "Having borne arms against the Russians for 10 years," he has said, "we think our battle with the Americans will be easy by comparison. . . ."

The fanaticism of bin Laden's closest followers and soldiers is also unlikely to wither away. "We spent a lot of time waiting to see [bin Laden] which gave us a chance to really sit around and talk with bin Laden's soldiers," said John Miller of America's *ABC News*, one of just a handful of Western journalists to have interviewed the al Qaeda leader. "They talked a great deal about the battles in Afghanistan, in Somalia, in other places where they've fought and their level of commitment to him. They regard him as almost a god."

BIN LADEN'S GROWING STRENGTH

Bin Laden's success following the US missile strikes was twofold. Firstly, he secured a large personal following throughout the Muslim world. Many who had never met him, whose only contact was through one of his interviews, a radio broadcast or Internet home-page, pronounced themselves ready to die for his cause. His second major success was to unify disparate groups of Islamic militants, even groups such as Islamic Jihad and the Islamic Group in Egypt, under his broad banner. Bin Laden's policy on this was clear: he views the Muslim world as a "single nation" with one religion, and points to the continued presence of American troops in Saudi Arabia, US support for Israel and the stalled peace process, and continued American action, both military and diplomatic, against Iraq, as reasons for fighting the US.

His influence within the militant Muslim world cannot be underestimated. Even among many moderate Muslims bin Laden is viewed with grudging respect as a man prepared to stand up to the arrogance of the world's only remaining superpower. Scores of Pakistanis have named their newborn sons Osama, while many others have actually changed the names of their sons to carry bin Laden's. Books about bin Laden and his beliefs have sold out in Pakistan, as have tens of thousands of stickers and pictures of the man. There is also the Osama Cloth House, the Osama Mosque and even the Osama Poultry Farm. It is some small indication of how the "cult" and legend of bin Laden is spreading around the world.

"Many Muslims see the American strikes against Afghanistan and Sudan as a huge arrogance of power," said Yousef al-Khoei, the influential head of the al-Khoei foundation, which represents the moderate face of Islam. "Muslims who carry out these attacks are the fringe. But those who applaud are the disenfranchised Muslims everywhere who see the double standard of the United States taking unilateral action against an Islamic nation. Now, anyone who stands up to the US becomes a hero."

NO MONOLITHIC ORGANIZATION

Some American experts agree. "Informed students of the subject have known for years that although the various militant Islamist movements around the world share a common ideology and many of the same grievances, they are not a monolithic international organization," according to Raymond

Close, a CIA veteran. The American attacks "may have inflamed their common zeal and hastened their unification and centralization—while probably adding hosts of new volunteers to their ranks. We are rolling up a big snowball." Close was right. By late 1998 more than twenty different militant factions were nestling under the broad umbrella of al Qaeda. Some of the most dangerous terrorists in the world were flocking to support bin Laden.

The U.S. Courts Indict Bin Laden and al Qaeda for Murder

United States District Court, Southern District of New York

The U.S. legal response to the 1998 African embassy attacks proved more effective than its military retaliation. In the press release reprinted here, the Manhattan Federal District Court announced the indictment of six men, including Osama bin Laden and his right-hand man, Mohammed Atef, for the attacks. In May 2001, four men were convicted on charges related to the bombings: Mohamed Rashed Daoud al-Owahli, Khalfan Khamis Mohammed, Wadih El-Hage, and Mohammed Sadiq Odeh. Osama bin Laden and Mohammed Atef remained at large. "Our job is not yet finished," commented U.S. attorney Mary Jo White at the time of the convictions. A far more deadly attack than the African bombings would soon bring Bin Laden's jihad to the U.S. homeland.

Mary Jo White, the United States Attorney for the Southern District of New York, and Lewis D. Schiliro, Assistant Director in Charge of the New York FBI Office, announced that Usama Bin Laden and Muhammad Atef, a/k/a "Abu Hafs," were indicted today in Manhattan federal court for the August 7, 1998, bombing of the United States embassies in Nairobi, Kenya, and Dar as Salaam, Tanzania, and for conspiring to kill American nationals outside of the United States.

The United States Department of State also announced today rewards of up to $5 million each for information leading to the arrest or conviction of Bin Laden and Atef.

The first court of the Indictment charges that Bin Laden and Atef, along with co-defendants Wadih El Hage, Fazul Abdullah Mohammed, Mohamed Sadeik Odeh, and Mohamed

United States District Court, Southern District of New York, press release, November 4, 1998.

Rashed Daoud Al-'Owhali, acted together with other members of "al Qaeda," a worldwide terrorist organization led by Bin Laden, in a conspiracy to murder United States nationals. The objectives of this international terrorist conspiracy allegedly included: killing members of the American military stationed in Saudi Arabia and Somalia; killing United States nationals employed at the United States Embassies in Nairobi, Kenya, and Dar es Salaam, Tanzania; and concealing the activities of the co-conspirators by, among other things, establishing front companies, providing false identity and travel documents, engaging in coded correspondence and providing false information to the authorities in various countries.

Bin Laden's organization al Qaeda allegedly functioned both on its own and through some of the terrorist organizations that operated under its umbrella, including the Al Jihad group based in Egypt, the Islamic Group (also known as "el Gamaa Islamia" or simply "Gamaa't"), led at one time by Sheik Omar Abdel Rahman, and a number of jihad groups in other countries, including the Sudan, Egypt, Saudi Arabia, Yemen and Somalia. Al Qaeda also allegedly maintained cells and personnel in a number of countries to facilitate its activities, including in Kenya, Tanzania, the United Kingdom and the United States.

According to the Indictment, Bin Laden and al Qaeda forged alliances with the National Islamic Front in the Sudan and with representatives of the government of Iran, and its associated terrorist group Hezballah, with the goal of working together against their perceived common enemies in the West, particularly the United States.

ACTIVITIES AND FATWAS

In order to further this international conspiracy to murder United States nationals, Bin Laden and other co-conspirators are alleged to have committed the following acts: (1) providing training camps for use by al Qaeda and its affiliates; (2) recruiting United States citizens including the defendant El Hage to help facilitate the goals of al Qaeda; (3) purchasing weapons and explosives; and (4) establishing headquarters and businesses in the Sudan.

The Indictment also alleges that *fatwahs* were issued by Bin Laden and a committee of al Qaeda members urging other members and associates of al Qaeda to kill Americans. According to the Indictment, several of these *fatwahs* called for attacks on American troops stationed in Saudi Arabia and Somalia. The Indictment also alleges that American troops in Somalia were indeed attacked and killed by persons who received training from al Qaeda members or those trained by al Qaeda. The Indictment specifically charges that the August 7, 1998, bombings of the United States embassies in Kenya and Tanzania as actions taken in furtherance of this conspiracy to kill American nationals.

Bin Laden and Atef, along with Abdullah Mohammed, Odeh, and Al-'Owhali, are also charged with bombing the two embassies and causing the deaths of more than 200 persons and injuring more than 4,500 others. Those five defendants are also charged with murdering all of the civilians killed in the embassy bombings. The Indictment names all of the victims of the bombings and each victim is charged as a separate count of murder for a total of 224 counts of murder against Bin Laden, Atef, Abdullah Mohammed, Odeh, and Al-'Owhali.

SENDING A MESSAGE TO TERRORISTS

Ms. White and Mr. Schiliro said the investigation of this case is being conducted by the Joint Terrorist Task Force composed of the FBI, the New York City Police Department, the United States Department of State, the United States Secret Service, the United States Immigration and Naturalization Service, the Federal Aviation Administration, the United States Marshals Service, the Bureau of Alcohol, Tobacco, and Firearms, the New York State Police and the Port Authority of New York and New Jersey.

Ms. White and Mr. Schiliro praised the Government of Kenya, Tanzania and the Comoros Islands for their cooperation in this investigation and praised all the investigative efforts and cooperation of the agencies involved in the case. They also said that the investigation is continuing.

United States Attorney General Janet Reno stated: "This is an important step forward in our fight against terrorism. It sends a message that no terrorist can flout our law and murder innocent civilians."

Ms. White stated: "Usama Bin Laden and his military commander Muhammad Atef are charged with the most heinous acts of violence ever committed against American diplomatic posts. These acts caused the deaths of hundreds of citizens of Kenya, Tanzania and the United States. All those responsible for these brutal and cowardly acts, from the leaders and organizers to all of those who had any role in these crimes in East Africa, will be brought to justice."

TO IDENTIFY, LOCATE, AND PROSECUTE

Mr. Schiliro stated: "This investigation has been given the highest priority. Our investigative strategy is clear: We will identify, locate and prosecute all those responsible right up the line, from those who constructed and delivered the bombs to those who paid for them and ordered it done. This has been an investigation which has involved the largest deployment of FBI agents abroad, including members of the Joint Terrorist Task Force. Working closely with the law enforcement authorities in Kenya and Tanzania, our investigators have made significant progress, yet much remains to be done."

Bin Laden and Atef, both of whom are fugitives, face a maximum sentence of life imprisonment without the possibility of parole, or death.

Assistant United States Attorney Patrick J. Fitzgerald, Kenneth M. Karas and Michael J. Garcia are in charge of the prosecution.

The charges contained in the Indictment are merely accusations, and the defendants are presumed innocent unless and until proven guilty.

The Bombing of the USS *Cole*

National Commission on Terrorist Attacks

On October 12, 2000, the destroyer USS *Cole* was in the port of Aden, Yemen, for a fuel stop. A small, manned boat approached the port side of the *Cole* and exploded. The suicide bombing caused a 40 by 40-foot gash in the side of the *Cole*, injuring 39 sailors and killing 17 others. The 9/11 Commission Report of 2004, excerpted here, relates how the attack was carried out, then describes the U.S. investigation that followed. The attack is now known to have been carried out by al Qaeda and supervised by Osama bin Laden himself. Revealingly, Bin Laden is believed to have been disappointed that the *Cole* bombing was not followed by a U.S. military strike. Nevertheless, the incident served as a propaganda coup for al Qaeda and helped its recruitment efforts.

[Al Qaeda's operational coordinators Tawfiq Attash Khallad and Abd al-Rahim al-Nashiri were both] involved during 1998 and 1999 in preparing to attack a ship off the coast of Yemen with a boatload of explosives. They had originally targeted a commercial vessel, specifically an oil tanker, but Bin Ladin urged them to look for a U.S. warship instead. In January 2000, their team had attempted to attack a warship in the port of Aden, but the attempt failed when the suicide boat sank. More than nine months later, on October 12, 2000, al Qaeda operatives in a small boat laden with explosives attacked a U.S. Navy destroyer, the USS *Cole*. The blast ripped a hole in the side of the *Cole*, killing 17 members of the ship's crew and wounding at least 40.

The plot, we now know, was a full-fledged al Qaeda operation, supervised directly by Bin Ladin. He chose the target

National Commission on Terrorists Attacks, *The 9/11 Commission Report: Final Report of the National Commission on Terrorist Attacks Upon the United States.* New York: W.W. Norton, 2004.

and location of the attack, selected the suicide operatives, and provided the money needed to purchase explosives and equipment. Nashiri was the field commander and managed the operation in Yemen. Khallad helped in Yemen until he was arrested in a case of mistaken identity and freed with Bin Ladin's help. . . . Local al Qaeda coordinators included Jamal al-Badawi and Fahd al Quso, who was supposed to film the attack from a nearby apartment. The two suicide operatives chosen were Hassan al Khamri and Ibrahim al Thawar, also known as Nibras. Nibras and Quso delivered money to Khallad in Bangkok [Thailand] during Khallad's January 2000 trip to Kuala Lumpur [Malaysia] and Bangkok.

In September 2000, Bin Ladin reportedly told Nashiri that he wanted to replace Khamri and Nibras. Nashiri was angry and disagreed, telling others he would go to Afghanistan and explain to Bin Ladin that the new operatives were already trained and ready to conduct the attack. Prior to departing, Nashiri gave Nibras and Khamri instructions to execute the attack on the next U.S. warship that entered the port of Aden.

While Nashiri was in Afghanistan, Nibras and Khamri saw their chance. They piloted the explosives-laden boat alongside the USS *Cole*, made friendly gestures to crew members, and detonated the bomb. Quso did not arrive at the apartment in time to film the attack.

A PROPAGANDA COUP

Back in Afghanistan, Bin Ladin anticipated U.S. military retaliation. He ordered the evacuation of al Qaeda's Kandahar airport compound and fled—first to the desert area near Kabul, then to Khowst and Jalalabad, and eventually back to Kandahar. In Kandahar, he rotated between five to six residences, spending one night at each residence. In addition, he sent his senior advisor, Mohammed Atef, to a different part of Kandahar and his deputy, Ayman al Zawahiri, to Kabul so that all three could not be killed in one attack.

There was no American strike. In February 2001, a source reported that an individual whom he identified as the big instructor (probably a reference to Bin Ladin) complained frequently that the United States had not yet attacked. According to the source, Bin Ladin wanted the United States to attack, and if it did not he would launch something bigger.

The attack on the USS *Cole* galvanized al Qaeda's recruitment efforts. Following the attack, Bin Ladin instructed the media committee, then headed by Khalid Sheikh Mohammed, to produce a propaganda video that included a reenactment of the attack along with images of the al Qaeda training camps and training methods; it also highlighted Muslim suffering in Palestine, Kashmir, Indonesia, and Chechnya. Al Qaeda's image was very important to Bin Ladin, and the video was widely disseminated. Portions were aired on Al Jazeera, CNN, and other television outlets. It was also disseminated among many young men in Saudi Arabia and Yemen, and caused many extremists to travel to Afghanistan for training and jihad. Al Qaeda members considered the video an effective tool in their struggle for preeminence among other Islamist and jihadist movements.

INVESTIGATING THE ATTACK

Teams from the FBI, the Naval Criminal Investigative Service, and the CIA were immediately sent to Yemen to investigate the attack. With difficulty, Barbara Bodine, the US. ambassador to Yemen, tried to persuade the Yemeni government to accept these visitors and allow them to carry arms, though the Yemenis balked at letting Americans openly carry long guns (rifles, shotguns, automatic weapons). Meanwhile, Bodine and the leader of the FBI team, John O'Neill, clashed repeatedly—to the point that after O'Neill had been rotated out of Yemen but wanted to return, Bodine refused the request. Despite the initial tension, the Yemeni and American investigations proceeded. Within a few weeks, the outline of the story began to emerge.

On the day of the *Cole* attack, a list of suspects was assembled that included al Qaeda's affiliate Egyptian Islamic Jihad. U.S. counterterrorism officials told us they immediately assumed that al Qaeda was responsible. But as Deputy DCI [Director of Central Intelligence] John McLaughlin explained to us, it was not enough for the attack to smell, look, and taste like an al Qaeda operation. To make a case, the CIA needed not just a guess but a link to someone known to be an al Qaeda operative.

Within the first weeks after the attack, the Yemenis found and arrested both Badawi and Quso, but did not let the FBI team participate in the interrogations. The CIA described initial Yemeni support after the *Cole* as "slow and inadequate." President [Bill] Clinton, Secretary [of State Madeleine] Albright, and DCI [George] Tenet all intervened to help. Because the information was secondhand, the U.S. team could not make its own assessment of its reliability.

IDENTIFYING KHALLAD

On November 11, the Yemenis provided the FBI with new information from the interrogations of Badawi and Quso, including descriptions of individuals from whom the detainees had received operational direction. One of them was Khallad, who was described as having lost his leg. The detainees said that Khallad helped direct the *Cole* operation from Afghanistan or Pakistan. The Yemenis (correctly) judged that the man described as Khallad was Tawfiq bin Attash.

An FBI special agent recognized the name Khallad and connected this news with information from an important al Qaeda source who had been meeting regularly with CIA and FBI officers. The source had called Khallad Bin Ladin's "run boy," and described him as having lost one leg in an explosives accident at a training camp a few years earlier. To confirm the identification, the FBI agent asked the Yemenis for their photo of Khallad. The Yemenis provided the photo on November 22, reaffirming their view that Khallad had been an intermediary between the plotters and Bin Ladin. (In a meeting with U.S. officials a few weeks later, on December 16, the source identified Khallad from the Yemeni photograph.)

U.S. intelligence agencies had already connected Khallad to al Qaeda terrorist operation, including the 1998 embassy bombings. By this time the Yemenis also had identified Nashiri, whose links to al Qaeda and the 1998 embassy bombings were even more well-known.

In other words, the Yemenis provided strong evidence connecting the *Cole* attack to al Qaeda during the second half of November, identifying individual operatives whom the United States knew were part of al Qaeda. During December the United States was able to corroborate this evidence. But the United States did not have evidence about Bin Ladin's personal involvement in the attacks until Nashiri and Khallad were captured in 2002 and 2003.

Connecting Bin Laden to the Attacks of September 11, 2001

The Government of the United Kingdom

On the morning of September 11, 2001, four American commercial aircraft were hijacked. Two were deliberately crashed into the twin towers of the World Trade Center in New York City, causing the buildings to collapse. Another was crashed into the Pentagon in Washington, D.C. Hijackers apparently intended the fourth airline to hit the White House, the U.S. Capitol, or Camp David, but a passenger revolt led to its crashing in a field near Shanksville, Pennsylvania. Almost immediately, Osama bin Laden and his al Qaeda network were suspected of responsibility for the attacks, which caused the deaths of 2,595 people. This suspicion was soon confirmed in a report by the British government, excerpted here.

1. The clear conclusions reached by the government are:
- Usama Bin Laden [UBL] and Al Qaida, the terrorist network which he heads, planned and carried out the atrocities on 11 September 2001;
- Usama Bin Laden and Al Qaida retain the will and resources to carry out further atrocities;
- the United Kingdom, and United Kingdom nationals are potential targets; and
- Usama Bin Laden and Al Qaida were able to commit these atrocities because of their close alliance with the Taleban régime, which allowed them to operate with impunity in pursuing their terrorist activity.

2. . . . The material in respect of 11 September comes from intelligence and the criminal investigation to date. The details of some aspects cannot be given, but the facts are clear from the intelligence.

The Government of the United Kingdom, "Responsibility for the Terrorist Atrocities in the United States, 11 September 2001: An Updated Account," www.number-10.gov.uk, 2001.

102

3. The document does not contain the totality of the material known to HMG [Her Majesty's Government], given the continuing and absolute need to protect intelligence sources.

BIN LADEN AND AL QAIDA

4. The relevant facts show:
- Al Qaida is a terrorist organisation with ties to a global network, which has been in existence for over 10 years. It was founded, and has been led at all times, by Usama Bin Laden.
- Usama Bin Laden and Al Qaida have been engaged in a jihad against the United States, and its allies. One of their stated aims is the murder of US citizens, and attacks on America's allies.
- Usama Bin Laden and Al Qaida have been based in Afghanistan since 1996, but have a network of operations throughout the world. The network includes training camps, warehouses, communication facilities and commercial operations able to raise significant sums of money to support its activity. That activity includes substantial exploitation of the illegal drugs trade from Afghanistan.
- Usama Bin Laden's Al Qaida and the Taleban régime have a close and mutually dependent alliance. Usama Bin Laden and Al Qaida provide the Taleban régime with material, financial and military support. They jointly exploit the drugs trade. The Taleban régime allows Bin Laden to operate his terrorist training camps and activities from Afghanistan, protects him from attacks from outside, and protects the drugs stockpiles. Usama Bin Laden could not operate his terrorist activities without the alliance and support of the Taleban régime. The Taleban's strength would be seriously weakened without Usama Bin Laden's military and financial support.
- Usama Bin Laden and Al Qaida have the capability to execute major terrorist attacks.
- Usama Bin Laden has claimed credit for the attack on US soldiers in Somalia in October 1993, which killed 18; for the attack on the US Embassies in Kenya and Tanzania in August 1998 which killed 224 and injured nearly 5000; and was linked to the attack on the USS *Cole* on 12 October 2000, in which 17 crew members were killed and 40 others injured.

- They have sought to acquire nuclear and chemical materials for use as terrorist weapons.

FEATURES IN COMMON

5. After 11 September we learned that, not long before, Bin Laden had indicated he was about to launch a major attack on America. The detailed planning for the terrorist attacks of 11 September was carried out by one of UBL's close associates. Of the 19 hijackers involved in 11 September 2001, it has been established that the majority had links with Al Qaida. A senior Bin Laden associate claimed to have trained some of the hijackers in Afghanistan. The attacks on 11 September 2001 were similar in both their ambition and intended impact to previous attacks undertaken by Usama Bin Laden and Al Qaida, and also had features in common. In particular:

- Suicide attackers
- Co-ordinated attacks on the same day
- The aim to cause maximum American casualties
- Total disregard for other casualties, including Muslim
- Meticulous long-term planning
- Absence of warning.

6. Al Qaida retains the capability and the will to make further attacks on the US and its allies, including the United Kingdom.

7. Al Qaida gives no warning of terrorist attack.

FACTS CONCERNING BIN LADEN AND THE TALEBAN

8. In 1989 Usama Bin Laden, and others, founded an international terrorist group known as "Al Qaida" (the Base). At all times he has been the leader of Al Qaida.

9. From 1989 until 1991 Usama Bin Laden was based in Afghanistan and Peshawar, Pakistan. In 1991 he moved to Sudan, where he stayed until 1996. In that year he returned to Afghanistan, where he remains.

10. The Taleban emerged from the Afghan refugee camps in Pakistan in the early 1990s. By 1996 they had captured Kabul. They are still engaged in a bloody civil war to control the whole of Afghanistan. They are led by Mullah Omar.

11. In 1996 Usama Bin Laden moved back to Afghanistan. He established a close relationship with Mullah Omar, and threw his support behind the Taleban. Usama Bin Laden and the Taleban régime have a close alliance on which both depend for their continued existence. They also share the

same religious values and vision.

12. Usama Bin Laden has provided the Taleban régime with troops, arms and money to fight the Northern Alliance. He is closely involved with Taleban military training, planning and operations. He has representatives in the Taleban military command structure. He has also given infrastruture assistance and humanitarian aid. Forces under the control of Usama Bin Laden have fought alongside the Taleban in the civil war in Afghanistan.

13. Omar has provided Bin Laden with a safe haven in which to operate, and has allowed him to establish terrorist training camps in Afghanistan. They jointly exploit the

---

INITIAL U.S. SUSPICIONS

Almost immediately after the attacks of September 11, 2001, suspicion fell upon Osama bin Laden and his al Qaeda network. On September 13, Secretary of State Colin Powell tentatively confirmed this suspicion in the following excerpts of a PBS interview with Jim Lehrer. Bin Laden's Saudi Arabian connections soon became a matter of growing concern to America.

JIM LEHRER: . . . There is no question that Osama bin Laden is a prime suspect, is that right?

COLIN POWELL: I think when you look at that region and when you examine the kinds of terrorist organizations around that have the sophistication to conduct such a series of attacks, you would certainly have to identify Osama bin Laden and his organization as being one of those suspects. . . .

JIM LEHRER: Now, the Saudis are very important in this, are they not, because bin Laden is a native of Saudi Arabia and his money comes from Saudi Arabia, does it not?

COLIN POWELL: Well, he's a native of Saudi Arabia, but I have to draw your attention to the very strong statement that the Saudi ambassador to the United States, Prince Bandar, made yesterday, which reminded everybody that his citizenship was taken away from him, bin Laden's citizenship was taken away from him; the Saudis consider him a disgrace to their nation and to his own heritage.

And they have condemned his actions. He has sources of money from various places throughout the world but I am absolutely confident that the Saudi government is not supporting his efforts in any way.

"Newsmaker: Colin Powell," *NewsHour with Jim Lehrer*, PBS, September 13, 2001. www.pbs.org.

Afghan drugs trade. In return for active Al Qaida support, the Taleban allow Al Qaida to operate freely, including planning, training and preparing for terrorist activity. In addition the Taleban provide security for the stockpiles of drugs.

U.S. OPPOSITION TO THE TALEBAN

14. Since 1996, when the Taleban captured Kabul, the United States government has consistently raised with them a whole range of issues, including humanitarian aid and terrorism. Well before 11 September 2001 they had provided evidence to the Taleban of the responsibility of Al Qaida for the terrorist attacks in East Africa. This evidence had been provided to senior leaders of the Taleban at their request.

15. The United States government had made it clear to the Taleban régime that Al Qaida had murdered US citizens, and planned to murder more. The US offered to work with the Taleban to expel the terrorists from Afghanistan. These talks, which have been continuing since 1996, have failed to produce any results.

16. In June 2001, in the face of mounting evidence of the Al Qaida threat, the United States warned the Taleban that it had the right to defend itself and that it would hold the régime responsible for attacks against US citizens by terrorists sheltered in Afghanistan.

17. In this, the United States had the support of the United Nations. The Security Council, in Resolution 1267, condemned Usama Bin Laden for sponsoring international terrorism and operating a network of terrorist camps, and demanded that the Taleban surrender Usama Bin Laden without further delay so that he could be brought to justice.

18. Despite the evidence provided by the US of the responsibility of Usama Bin Laden and Al Qaida for the 1998 East Africa bombings, despite the accurately perceived threats of further atrocities, and despite the demands of the United Nations, the Taleban régime responded by saying no evidence existed against Usama Bin Laden, and that neither he nor his network would be expelled.

19. A former Government official in Afghanistan has described the Taleban and Usama Bin Laden as "two sides of the same coin: Usama cannot exist in Afghanistan without the Taleban and the Taleban cannot exist without Usama".

20. Al Qaida is dedicated to opposing "un-Islamic" governments in Muslim countries with force and violence.

21. Al Qaida virulently opposes the United States. Usama Bin Laden has urged and incited his followers to kill American citizens, in the most unequivocal terms.

22. On 12 October 1996 he issued a declaration of jihad as follows:

"The people of Islam have suffered from aggression, iniquity and injustice imposed by the Zionist-Crusader alliance and their collaborators. . . .

"It is the duty now on every tribe in the Arabian peninsula to fight jihad and cleanse the land from these Crusader occupiers. Their wealth is booty to those who kill them.

"My Muslim brothers: your brothers in Palestine and in the land of the two Holy Places [Saudi Arabia] *are calling upon your help and asking you to take part in fighting against the enemy—the Americans and the Israelis. They are asking you to do whatever you can to expel the enemies out of the sanctities of Islam."*

Later in the same year he said that

"terrorising the American occupiers [of Islamic holy places] *is a religious and logical obligation".*

FATWA AND OTHER STATEMENTS

In February 1998 he issued and signed a "fatwa" [holy declaration] which included a decree to all Muslims:

". . . the killing of Americans and their civilian and military allies is a religious duty for each and every Muslim to be carried out in whichever country they are until Al Aqsa mosque [in Jerusalem] *has been liberated from their grasp and until their armies have left Muslim lands."*

In the same "fatwa" he called on Muslim scholars and their leaders and their youths to

"launch an attack on the American soldiers of Satan"

and concluded:

"We—with God's help—call on every Muslim who believes in God and wishes to be rewarded to comply with God's order to kill Americans and plunder their money whenever and wherever they find it. We also call on Muslims . . . to launch the raid on Satan's US troops and the devil's supporters allying with them, and to displace those who are behind them."

When asked, in 1998, about obtaining chemical or nuclear weapons he said *"acquiring such weapons for the defence of Muslims [is] a religious duty"*, and made the following claim in an interview printed in the Pakistan newspaper *Dawn* in November 2001:

"I wish to declare that if America used chemical or nuclear weapons against us, then we may retort with chemical and nuclear weapons. We have the weapons as deterrent."

In an interview aired on Al Jazira (Doha, Qatar) television he stated:

"Our enemy is every American male, whether he is directly fighting us or paying taxes."

In two interviews broadcast on US television in 1997 and 1998 he referred to the terrorists who carried out the earlier attack on the World Trade Center in 1993 as *"role models"*. He went on to exhort his followers *"to take the fighting to America"*.

THE THREAT TO U.S. ALLIES

23. From the early 1990s Usama Bin Laden has sought to obtain nuclear and chemical materials for use as weapons of terror.

24. Although US targets are Al Qaida's priority, it also explicitly threatens the United States' allies. References to *"Zionist-Crusader alliance and their collaborators"*, and to *"Satan's US troops and the devil's supporters allying with them"* are references which unquestionably include the United Kingdom. This is confirmed by more specific references in a broadcast of 13 October, during which Bin Laden's spokesman said:

"Al Qaida declares that Bush Sr, Bush Jr, Clinton, Blair and Sharon are the arch-criminals from among the Zionists and Crusaders . . . Al Qaida stresses that the blood of those killed

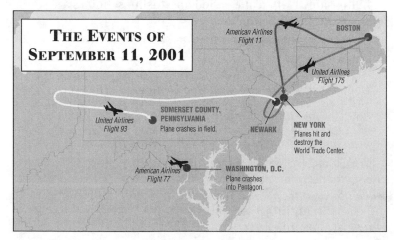

THE EVENTS OF SEPTEMBER 11, 2001

American Airlines Flight 11

BOSTON

United Airlines Flight 175

United Airlines Flight 93

SOMERSET COUNTY, PENNSYLVANIA
Plane crashes in field.

NEWARK

NEW YORK
Planes hit and destroy the World Trade Center.

American Airlines Flight 77

WASHINGTON, D.C.
Plane crashes into Pentagon.

*will not go to waste, God willing, until we punish these crimi-
nals . . . We also say and advise the Muslims in the United
States and Britain . . . not to travel by plane. We also advise
them not to live in high-rise buildings and towers."*

25. There is a continuing threat. Based on our experience
of the way the network has operated in the past, other cells,
like those that carried out the terrorist attacks on 11 September, must be assumed to exist.

26. Al Qaida functions both on its own and through a network of other terrorist organisations. These include Egyptian Islamic Jihad and other north African Islamic extremist
terrorist groups, and a number of other jihadi groups in
other countries including the Sudan, Yemen, Somalia, Pakistan and India. Al Qaida also maintains cells and personnel
in a number of other countries to facilitate its activities.

27. Usama Bin Laden heads the Al Qaida network. Below
him is a body known as the Shura, which includes representatives of other terrorist groups, such as Egyptian Islamic Jihad leader Ayman Zawahiri and prominent lieutenants of
Bin Laden such as Mohamed Atef (also known as Abu Hafs
Al-Masri). Egyptian Islamic Jihad has, in effect, merged with
Al Qaida.

28. In addition to the Shura, Al Qaida has several groups
dealing with military, media, financial and Islamic issues.

29. Mohamed Atef is a member of the group that deals
with military and terrorist operations. His duties include
principal responsibility for training Al Qaida members.

30. Members of Al Qaida must make a pledge of allegiance to follow the orders of Usama Bin Laden.

31. A great deal of evidence about Usama Bin Laden and
Al Qaida has been made available in the US indictment for
earlier crimes.

BIN LADEN'S FINANCIAL DEALINGS

32. Since 1989, Usama Bin Laden has conducted substantial
financial and business transactions on behalf of Al Qaida
and in pursuit of its goals. These include purchasing land for
training camps, purchasing warehouses for the storage of
items, including explosives, purchasing communications
and electronics equipment, and transporting currency and
weapons to members of Al Qaida and associated terrorist
groups in countries throughout the world.

33. Since 1989 Usama Bin Laden has provided training

camps and guest houses in Afghanistan, Pakistan, the Sudan, Somalia and Kenya for the use of Al Qaida and associated terrorist groups. We know from intelligence that there are currently at least a dozen camps across Afghanistan, of which at least four are used for training terrorists.

34. Since 1989, Usama Bin Laden has established a series of businesses to provide income for Al Qaida, and to provide cover for the procurement of explosives, weapons and chemicals, and for the travel of Al Qaida operatives. The businesses have included a holding company known as "Wadi Al Aqiq," a construction business known as "Al Hijra," an agricultural business known as "Al Themar Al Mubaraka," and investment companies known as "Ladin International" and "Taba Investments.". . .

61. Nineteen men have been identified as the hijackers from the passenger lists of the four planes hijacked on 11 September 2001. Many of them had previous links with Al Qaida or have so far been positively identified as associates of Al Qaida. An associate of some of the hijackers has been identified as playing key roles in both the East African Embassy attacks and the USS *Cole* attack. Investigations continue into the backgrounds of all the hijackers.

62. From intelligence sources, the following facts have been established subsequent to 11 September; for intelligence reasons, the names of associates, though known, are not given.

- In the run-up to 11 September, Bin Laden was mounting a concerted propaganda campaign amongst like-minded groups of people—including videos and documentation—justifying attacks on Jewish and American targets; and claiming that those who died in the course of them were carrying out God's work.
- We have learned, subsequent to 11 September, that Bin Laden himself asserted shortly before 11 September that he was preparing a major attack on America.
- In August and early September close associates of Bin Laden were warned to return to Afghanistan from other parts of the world by 10 September.
- Immediately prior to 11 September some known associates of Bin Laden were naming the date for action as on or around 11 September.
- A senior associate claimed to have trained some of the hijackers in Afghanistan.
- Since 11 September we have learned that one of Bin

Laden's closest and most senior associates was responsible for the detailed planning of the attacks.

- There is evidence of a very specific nature relating to the guilt of Bin Laden and his associates that is too sensitive to release.

SELF-INCRIMINATING LANGUAGE

63. In addition, Usama Bin Laden has issued a number of public statements since the US strikes on Afghanistan began. The language used in these, while not an open admission of guilt, is self-incriminating.

64. For example, on 7 October he said:

"Here is America struck by God Almighty in one of its vital organs, so that its greatest buildings are destroyed. Grace and gratitude to God . . . I swear to God that America will not live in peace before peace reigns in Palestine, and before all the army of infidels depart the land of Mohammed, peace be upon him."

65. On 9 October his spokesman praised the *"good deed"* of the hijackers, who *"transferred the battle into the US heartland."* He warned that the *"storm of plane attacks will not abate."*

66. On 20 October Bin Laden gave an inflammatory interview which has been circulating, in the form of a video, among supporters in the Al Qaida network. In the transcript, when referring to the US buildings that were attacked, he says:

"It is what we instigated for a while, in self-defence. And it was in revenge for our people killed in Palestine and Iraq. So if avenging the killing of our people is terrorism, let history be a witness that we are terrorists."

Later in the interview he said:

"Bush and Blair . . . don't understand any language but the language of force. Every time they kill us, we will kill them, so the balance of terror can be achieved."

He went on:

"The battle has been moved inside America, and we shall continue until we win this battle, or die in the cause and meet our maker."

He also said:

"The bad terror is what America and Israel are practising against our people, and what we are practising is the good terror that will stop them doing what they are doing."

67. Usama Bin Laden remains in charge, and the mastermind, of Al Qaida. In Al Qaida, an operation on the scale of

the 11 September attacks would have been approved by Usama Bin Laden himself.

68. The modus operandi of 11 September was entirely consistent with previous attacks. Al Qaida's record of atrocities is characterised by meticulous long-term planning, a desire to inflict mass casualties, suicide bombers, and multiple simultaneous attacks.

69. The attacks of 11 September 2001 are entirely consistent with the scale and sophistication of the planning which went into the attacks on the East African Embassies and the USS *Cole*. No warnings were given for these three attacks, just as there was none on 11 September.

70. Al Qaida operatives, in evidence given in the East African Embassy bomb trials, have described how the group spends years preparing for an attack. They conduct repeated surveillance, patiently gather materials, and identify and vet operatives, who have the skills to participate in the attack and the willingness to die for their cause.

71. The operatives involved in the 11 September atrocities attended flight schools, used flight simulators to study the controls of larger aircraft and placed potential airports and routes under surveillance.

72. Al Qaida's attacks are characterised by total disregard for innocent lives, including Muslims. In an interview after the East African bombings, Usama Bin Laden insisted that the need to attack the United States excused the killing of other innocent civilians, Muslim and non-Muslim alike.

73. No other organisation has both the motivation and the capability to carry out attacks like those of the 11 September—only the Al Qaida network under Usama Bin Laden.

A DEADLY ALLIANCE

74. The attacks of the 11 September 2001 were planned and carried out by Al Qaida, an organisation whose head is Usama Bin Laden. That organisation has the will, and the resources, to execute further attacks of similar scale. Both the United States and its close allies are targets for such attacks. The attack could not have occurred without the alliance between the Taleban and Usama Bin Laden, which allowed Bin Laden to operate freely in Afghanistan, promoting, planning and executing terrorist activity.

Distorting the Word *Jihad*

Esther Sakinah Quinlan

After the attacks of September 11, 2001, the word *jihad* was on the lips of people all over the world. Partly because Osama bin Laden had declared jihad against the enemies of Islam, the word was commonly assumed to mean "holy war." But this is a mistranslation of a subtle and powerful concept. In response to the attacks, the converted Muslim Esther Sakinah Quinlan wrote the following article for *Tikkun* magazine. In it, she contrasts true jihad as described in mainstream Islamic thought against the distorted concept of jihad advocated by Bin Laden and other Islamic militants. Quinlan teaches in the program of writing and rhetoric at the University of Colorado in Boulder.

Most Americans have some image from September 11 that has stayed with them during the year since the attacks. Mine was not a television image. It was a single line of print: "One of the hijackers left a Qur'an in his rental car at Logan Airport." When I read it, I felt indignant and sad. I wondered if other Americans would draw the conclusion that this criminal had been reading the Qur'an to find justification for the crime he was about to commit. Trying to be optimistic, I told myself that "everyone *knows* the distortion of religious ideals is not new or unique to Islam; everyone *knows* that all religions have been used to mask naked aggression." Yet, accurate as these observations are, how persuasive are they compared to the image of Osama bin Laden stroking an AK47 and saying that jihâd is legitimate against all Americans? He and others like him believe that the Qur'an supports their understanding of jihâd. Even Muslims who reject terrorism have beliefs about jihâd that are unsettling.

Esther Sakinah Quinlan, "The Jihad Question," *Tikkun*, September/October 2002. Copyright © 2002 by Institute for Labor and Mental Health. Copyright © 2002 by *Tikkun*: A Bimonthly Jewish Critique of Politics, Culture & Society. Reproduced by permission.

The emotive power of the word *jihâd* was shown at Harvard's commencement this year. Zayed Yasin, a graduating senior, was to deliver a speech entitled "Of Faith and Citizenship: My American Jihad." Many of his fellow students fervently opposed the administration's choice of speaker and his subject. They asked the university to remove him from the program.

At this time, when peace activists feel discouraged and face formidable obstacles in the United States and abroad, an accurate understanding of jihâd could open up a new avenue for discourse with Muslims.

THE POWER OF THE QUR'AN

The word "*qur'an*" means *recitation.* Muslims believe that the Qur'an was communicated from God to Muhammad through a mysterious process, with the Angel Gabriel as the intermediary. This is why Muhammad, like Moses, Jesus, and Abraham, is known as a Messenger of God. Muhammad received and transmitted the Qur'anic revelations as they came to him over a period of twenty-three years.

The Qur'an has a power, a kind of grace, known as *baraka,* which is impossible to analyze logically. Memorizing and reciting its verses is a sacred act because, as Professor Sayyed Hossein Nasr explains in his *Ideas and Realities of Islam,* the Divine presence in the text provides food for the souls of human beings. In more conventional terms, we can say that the Qur'an is not a "book" in the ordinary sense because its very words are considered sacred. Westerners, who tend not to respect the power of sacred language, can find such reverence puzzling.

The word *jihâd* comes from the verb *jahada:* to struggle, to make an effort, and, by extension, to fight in defense of the faith. Some form of the word appears forty-one times in the Qur'an. Here are a few examples: "Seek the means to come to Him, and struggle in His way" (5:35); "Struggle in God's way with your possessions and your selves" (9:41) and "those who struggle in Our Cause, surely We shall guide them" (29:69).

The expression "struggle in God's way" has both an inner and an outer meaning. The struggle to be a good person and to draw near to God is the inner jihâd. Muhammad called it the greater jihâd, the *jihâd al-akbar.* The lesser jihâd is actual combat. Terrorism is not jihâd. Muslim jurists distinguish four ways to fulfill the duty to struggle: by the heart, by the tongue, by the hands, and by the sword. Different though the word seems from the Hebrew word *tikkun* [restoration or universal correction], jihâd does have the sense of transforming and putting things right, restoring goodness, order, and justice—restoring those qualities which the Creator meant life in this world to have. When *genuine* jihâd results in these things, healing has occurred.

THE QUR'AN AND EXTREMISTS

Terrorists and radicals have their own sense of what jihâd means. In a way, extremist "Islamism" is like other "isms"; it is a kind of millennialism. These people yearn for a perfect world, a "pure Islam." They yearn for an end to suffering and injustice; they yearn to topple the imperial powers that they see as the agents of evil. To generate combative, manic energy, they frame the entire world in dualistic terms of light and darkness. They see the United States as king of the forces of darkness because it has the most power and money.

It can be very hard for Americans to understand why these fundamentalists—and sometimes even their more moderate co-religionists—hate us, our culture, and our international policies that have left huge footprints in their world.

Psychologically, Muslims are reacting to a collective humiliation and feeling of powerlessness that can be traced to a steady eight-hundred-year decline in the scope and power of the Muslim world—a decline which the West has manipulated to its advantage. Muslims were once a very proud people with a society advanced in the arts, science, and social organization. At the time of the Crusades, Muslims regarded the crusaders as total barbarians, with some reason. But gradually the Islamic Empire weakened and Western powers reduced the Muslim states to colonies. After World War I, Western powers again carved up the Middle East in ways that served to further their own power. The UN's creation of Israel in 1948 and the Arab's defeat in the 1967 Six Day War left no doubt about how powerless Arab Muslims had become.

After Arab-Muslim countries finally won their independence from the West, they tried to reassert themselves through Marxism, then Nationalism—both of which failed. Those failures led Arab Muslims to turn to their own indigenous culture: the culture and religion of Islam; this turning has led them to seek in the Qur'an verses which validate their hurt and hold the promise of restoring self-respect. The anger that they feel at their continuing failure to succeed politically and economically becomes displaced and projected onto the West.

Because extremists use the Qur'an to justify their views, those who wish to understand Islam must take a short course in Qur'anic interpretation. Just as the Judeo-Christian Bible can be used by both the Left and Right, the Qur'an is susceptible to radically different readings.

THE TEACHINGS OF SAYYID QUTB

One of the most influential figures in radical Islam is Sayyid Qutb, an Egyptian activist in the 1950s, who argued in favor of confronting all non-Islamic power structures with physical force. Even existing "Islamic" states became potential targets. Qutb's book, *Milestones*, epitomizes radical Islam. Even some moderates who reject terrorism respect him as a martyr.

The pages of *Milestones* crackle with the fire of millennialism. Qutb writes that the purpose of Islam's coming into history is "to proclaim the authority and sovereignty of God . . . to eliminate all human kingship, and to announce the rule of the Sustainer of the universe over the entire earth." The fact that the Sustainer of the universe already has authority over all of creation seems to have escaped him. But projecting perfection into the future characterizes millennialist thinking.

Sayyid Qutb believes that "Islam is a declaration of the freedom of every man or woman from servitude to other humans." How will this heady freedom happen? Qutb says that Islam will take the initiative (read "hostile action") because

> it has the right to destroy all obstacles in the form of institutions and traditions that restrict man's freedom of choice. It does not attack individuals nor does it force them to accept its beliefs. It attacks institutions and traditions in order to release human beings from the pernicious influence which distorts human nature and curtails human freedom.

QUR'ANIC JUSTIFICATION FOR DESTRUCTION

What then is Sayyid Qutb's Qur'anic justification for such destruction, for such a radical vision of jihåd? He and other thinkers claim that the Qur'anic verses promoting liberation of the oppressed are a carte blanche for destruction. What of

Qur'anic verses advocating restraint? Qutb draws his answer from Islamic history. In the early days of the Prophet's mission, Qutb argues, Muhammed had no armed forces; therefore, God prescribed restraint, patience, and the making of treaties with unbelievers, Jews, and others. It was during this period that the verses forbidding the initiation of jihâd were revealed. However, when the Muslim community was secure in Medina in the later years of the Prophet's life, verse 9:29 was revealed.

> And fight those who have not faith in God,
> Nor in the Hereafter, and [who] forbid not
> What God and His Prophet have forbidden,
> And [who] are not committed to the religion of
> Truth among those who have been given the Book,
> Until they pay the tribute and are humbled.

Qutb and those Muslims who believe that the above verse authorizes an on-going jihâd look back to a mist-shrouded Golden Age—to the time when Islam ruled most of two continents and when non-Muslims were required to pay a small but symbolic tax. The reference to humbling (literally *made small*) soothes the sense of powerlessness and humiliation that many Arab Muslims feel. At the same time, the reference also upsets Americans because of our ideals of equality before the law and the separation of religion and law. Not reacting with aggression or denigration to this view severely stretches and tests our capacity for tolerance. Because the stakes are so high now, we must understand and not demonize those who test us. If we demonize them, we make them more powerful.

THE QUR'AN AND MODERATES

In contrast to the historical and literalist interpretations of Muslim extremists lies the interpretive practice of moderate Muslims and the Sufis, who represent the esoteric, mystical dimension of Islam. In contrast to the extremists, when moderate Muslims, and especially the Sufis, read the Qur'an, they understand that the accounts of the prophets are not just historical. They are also accounts of the struggle in each human soul. While terrorists like Qutb read the Qur'an literally or as an external political allegory, moderates will read the Qur'an as an internal allegory of the soul. For example, extremists read Moses' confrontation with Pharaoh, ironically, as a political allegory for the Muslims' confrontation with the United States (and the Jews!). Moderates, on the other hand, tend to read Pharoah as representing an inner evil that we must work to overcome.

Moderates and Sufis also take a different approach from the extremists when it comes to interpretive dilemmas. Ex-

THE LEGEND OF BIN LADEN BEGINS

International correspondent Mary Anne Weaver was covering the Soviet-Afghan war when Osama bin Laden's name first began to be known. In the following excerpt from an article for The New Yorker, *Weaver relates how she first heard of America's future enemy. Weaver's books include* A Portrait of Egypt: A Journey Through the World of Militant Islam *and* Pakistan: In the Shadow of Jihad and Afghanistan.

In 1984, bin Laden moved to Peshawar, a Pakistani border town near the Khyber Pass which served as the key staging area for the jihad in Afghanistan. That year, I and other journalists in the region began to hear of a man known as the Good Samaritan or the Saudi Prince. He would arrive unannounced, it was said, at hospitals where wounded Afghan and Arab fighters had been brought. He was lean and elegant, and dressed in the traditional *shalwar kameez* of the Afghan tribes—a blousy knee-length tunic top—over tailored trousers of fine English cloth, and he always wore English custom-made Beal Brothers boots. According to the stories that we heard, he was soft-spoken, and went from bed to bed dispensing cashews and English chocolates to the wounded and carefully noting each man's name and address. Weeks later, the man's family would receive a generous check.

Soon we began to hear other tales. In the ungovernable tribal areas on the Pakistani-Afghan frontier, and in the military training camps outside Peshawar and in Afghanistan, jihad trainees and clerics began to speak of another enigmatic Saudi. He had arrived in an unmarked military transport plane, and brought in bulldozers and other pieces of heavy equipment, which he deployed to design and construct defensive tunnels and storage depots, and to cut roads through the deep valleys of Afghanistan. According to one frequently told story, the man often drove one of the bulldozers himself across the precipitous mountain peaks, exposing himself to strafing from Soviet helicopter gunships. This man also turned out to be bin Laden, and the equipment that he brought in was furnished by the Bin Laden Group.

Mary Anne Weaver, "The Real bin Laden," *The New Yorker*, January 24, 2000.

tremists tend to disregard verses that contradict verses that support their goals. Moderates and Sufis, on the other hand, both agree that all verses on a particular issue must be examined before making any determination about which verse to follow. In particular, this way of reading the Qur'an is based on the principle that an interpretation of a verse is valid *only* if it does not contradict another verse in the Qur'an. Application of this principle prevents the distortion that occurs by taking quotations out of context.

To better understand this all-important principle, we can turn to the work of Iranian scholar Ayatollah Mutaharri, who has demonstrated in his lectures (available online at www.al-islam.org/short/jihad) the intellectual and religious dishonesty of using the Qur'an to justify terrorism and murder. Readers may wonder at the validity of using an Iranian scholar for this purpose when Iran itself waged a ghastly and ultimately futile nine-year "jihad" against Iraq. Although the Iranian government is overseen by religious authorities, not all religious scholars can be manipulated to say what the state wants them to say. Mutahhari is respected for the independence and integrity of his arguments.

CONDITIONAL AND UNCONDITIONAL COMMANDS

Both Qur'anic scholars like Mutaharri (and Sufis such as the poet Rumi) differentiate between conditional verses and unconditional verses. According to Mutaharri, "when both an unconditional and a conditional command exist, i.e., when there is an instruction that in one place is unconditional but in another place has a condition attached, then . . . the unconditional [one] must be interpreted [in light of] the conditional [one]." In other words, when Muslims cite verses that command them to fight, they must interpret those verses *together with* other verses that restrict fighting to specific circumstances. Here is an example of this method of interpretation.

Extremists like bin Laden and Qutb quote *unconditional* verses about fighting, verses such as this one: "slay them [enemies] wherever you find them" (4:89) or this one: "O Prophet, fight against the unbelievers and hypocrites and be stern against them" (9:73). (The verb in these verse in *qatala*, to fight, slay.) Terrorists cite this type of verse because it suits their political purpose. According to the scholars like Mutaharri, however, taking verses out of context is an illegitimate way to use the Qur'an. Thus, the command to fight against unbelievers is qualified by the command that permits fighting against those who begin aggression. "Defend yourself against your enemies, but do not attack them first; God hates the aggressor" (2:190). No permission is given to fight or kill anyone except those who begin the aggression.

There are two other situations in which actual fighting is permitted. The first case directly involves religion and religious practice. The Qur'an explicitly forbids compelling anyone to adopt a religion. "There is no compulsion in religion" (2:256). At the same time, other people do not have the right to forbid people from being Muslims. Doing so is considered a form of aggression. Yet even when Muslims find their faith under attack, says Ayatollah Mutahhari and other authorities, "It is not permissible for us to fight with that nation, with those people who are blameless and unaware. Nevertheless, it is permissible for us to fight against that corrupt regime."

AN OBLIGATION TO FIGHT

The second Qur'anic condition that makes the use of force valid is the obligation to fight those who oppress others. The Qur'an says: "Permission is given [for warfare] to those who have been attacked and definitely wronged." (22:39) Coming to the aid of victims of injustice, regardless of their religion, is an obligation. This idea is identical to the Christian concept of the just war. It is also part of America's justification for intervention in Bosnia and Kosovo, in World War II, and now in Afghanistan.

Sayyed Hossein Nasr, in *Islam and the Question of Violence*, writes that

> Even in war . . . the inflicting of any injury to women, and children is forbidden, as is the use of force against civilians. Only fighters in the field of battle must be confronted with force, and it is only against them that injurious physical force can be used. Inflicting injuries outside of the context . . . is completely forbidden by Islamic Law.

Muhammad, the Messenger of God, would now allow his soldiers to fight when he returned in triumph with an army to Mecca, the city that had driven him and his followers out. Many enemies of Islam remained there. But because believers were mixed together with unbelievers, and civilians were mixed with warriors, he forbade combat. The terrorists who attacked the World Trade Center—where only civilians worked, and where there certainly was a mixture of believers and non-believers—ignored not only the Qur'an guidelines, but also Muhammad's example.

OFFERING PEACE

The Qur'an advocates peace and reconciliation whenever possible. It says that "peace is better" (4:128) and "O you who have found faith, enter peace wholly" (2:20), and, even more to the point, "And if they incline to peace, then you incline to it" (8:61). Perhaps the most important verse about peace is this one: "Thus, if they let you be, and do not make war on you, and offer peace, God does not allow you to harm them" (4:90). When peace is *not* possible, the sacred text places clear conditions on the use of force in order to control the human inclination to be unjust and aggressive.

The situation in seventh-century Arabia was not really so different from our world today. As we know, aggression and injustice require a response. Sometimes that response includes combat. The Qur'anic principles regarding the regulation of combat are designed to (1) limit and control the use of force in order to restore justice, (2) permit self-defense, and (3) when necessary, protect the free practice of religion.

ISRAEL

The subject of terrorism and jihâd cannot be separated from the current situation in Palestine. . . . To Arab Muslims still pained by the wounds of colonialism, Israel is an European-American colony in the midst of an Arab nation. To them, Israel represents their greatest failure. It is a constant reminder of their lack of power. Almost all the [Arab] suicide bombers have a personal reason that supports their insane act: the death, maiming, or imprisonment of a loved one at enemy hands. For them, the general feeling of humiliation and powerlessness has materialized in a concrete way. A high percentage of these suicides seems to be more of a personal act than a religious one.

For ordinary Muslims who are not extremists, Palestine is a collective wound. They feel that they cannot turn their backs on their suffering brothers and sisters there, the religious bond being stronger than the national bond. They relate these lines from the Qur'an to the Palestinians:

> Why should you not fight in the cause of God when weak
> men, women, and children are imploring; "Our Lord, deliver
> us from this community whose people are oppressive" (4:75).

Taking these lines completely out of context, bin Laden saw the September 11 terror as a strike against Israel as well. Few Arab Muslims have taken that extremist position. Many, however, while condemning the September 11 attacks, have coupled their condemnation with reference to the injustice the Palestinians endure. For example, Shaykh al-Qaradawi calls the September 11 acts a "heinous crime in Islam," but goes on to suggest that the Palestinian attacks on Israel belong to a different category: The category covered by the verse that sanctions fighting to liberate those who are oppressed.

Suicide as a Method of Jihad

To support suicide bombings, pro-terrorist Muslims quote this verse:

> Those who fight in the cause of God are those who forsake this world in favor of the Hereafter. Whoever fights in the cause of God and then is killed, or attains victory, We [God] will surely grant him a great recompense (4:74).

Here again, we need to apply the basic principle of Qur'anic interpretation: that one interpretation must not contradict another. In two verses (17:33 and 4:29) the Qur'an, by implication, condemns suicide. In 2:195, it does so explicitly: "Cast not yourselves into destruction by your own hand." Therefore, the above verse concerning the reward for martyrdom cannot be interpreted in a vacuum. It must be tempered and reinterpreted along side the Qur'anic prohibition against taking one's own life.

Besides, common sense tells us that suicide is not a way to fight, nor does it leave to God the option of whether one lives or dies during battle. It is a taking of one's life in one's own hands, an act which usurps the right belonging to Him alone who gave that life. In addition, suicide bombings are designed to kill innocent civilians, an act expressly forbidden by the Qur'an. For these two reasons, suicide as a method of jihâd cannot be justified according to Islamic principles, as moderates understand them.

The Sacred Mosaic

It is natural to ask, "Why didn't God just put all the guidelines about jihâd together in one place in His Book and arrange it so that there is no room for misunderstanding? If IIe had done that, then the hijackers piloting their planes into the World Trade Center could not have looked to the Qur'an for support." Another Sufi scholar, Frithjof Schuon, has an answer. He explains that "A sacred text with its seeming contradictions and obscurities is . . . like a mosaic, or even an anagram." Because of this divine design, only a holistic hermeneutics will do.

This mosaic design of a sacred text tests those who look to it for truth. Whatever our faith, we want truth to be easy to grasp; we want our sacred texts to read like a clear textbook. But they do not. In fact, as Christians and Jews well know, sacred texts are difficult. Pope Pius XII said that God has made them this way "in order that we may be stimulated to read and study them with greater attention."

Today, we must do more than read and study our sacred texts. We are in the grip of huge historical forces. In order to carry the Light in the Darkness of these times, we can do several things. We can refuse to accept a hate-filled reading of the Qur'anic concept of jihâd and refuse to demonize Muslims.

On the political level, we can pressure leaders to see that it is not in America's best interest to support repressive Middle Eastern regimes or regimes which exclude all Islamic parties from the political process. Such policies provide terrorists the hooks on which to hang their millenialist projections.

THE NEED FOR DIALOGUE

Offering secularism as the antidote to religious violence, as some journalists propose, plays into the hands of those who see their role as combatants, "soldiers of God" in the fight against atheist rule. The infiltration of secularism into the Muslim world ignites feelings of humiliation and powerlessness. To most Muslims, religion and culture are a single package. However, the primary responsibility for intervention rests with Muslims themselves. Islam contains within it the means to correct the distorted use of its holy book. Consultation (*shur'ah*) is encouraged in Islam. Muslims must counter the terrorists' perverted use of the Qur'an—not directly—but through education and dialogue. Some of this is happening, but not nearly enough. In some places, challenging the extremists endangers one's life. It may well be that North American converts to Islam and immigrant Muslims, who are free to speak out without risk here, should shoulder much of this responsibility. What Muslims are thinking and believing here filters back to the countries the immigrants came from.

In addition, there is a role for Americans of other faiths. Inviting Muslims to engage in dialogue can be invaluable for both parties. True dialogue is not just the exchange of viewpoints. The information exchanged is secondary to the recognition of the divine heart in all people. Every time this happens, the forces of darkness are reduced a little.

CHAPTER 4

THE HUNT FOR BIN LADEN

PEOPLE WHO MADE HISTORY

OSAMA BIN LADEN

Escape from Tora Bora

Barton Gellman and Thomas E. Ricks

After the attacks of September 11, 2001, Afghanistan's Taliban government refused to turn Osama bin Laden over to the United States. Assisted by the Northern Alliance, longtime enemies of the Taliban, the United States and its allies invaded Afghanistan in October 2001. The Taliban was soon defeated and removed from power. For a time, it seemed possible that Osama bin Laden had perished in the fighting, but it eventually became evident that the al Qaeda leader was still alive. The following year, the administration of President George W. Bush determined that U.S. forces had missed an opportunity to capture or kill Bin Laden during the battle for Tora Bora in December 2001. The following news story of April 17, 2002, written for the *Washington Post* by Barton Gellman and Thomas E. Ricks, details the reasons for this failure. Gellman and Ricks were part of a *Washington Post* team that won a 2002 Pulitzer Prize for coverage of America's war on terrorism.

The Bush administration has concluded that Osama bin Laden was present during the battle for Tora Bora late last year and that failure to commit U.S. ground troops to hunt him was its gravest error in the war against al Qaeda, according to civilian and military officials with first-hand knowledge.

Intelligence officials have assembled what they believe to be decisive evidence, from contemporary and subsequent interrogations and intercepted communications, that bin Laden began the battle of Tora Bora inside the cave complex along Afghanistan's mountainous eastern border. Though there remains a remote chance that he died there, the intelligence community is persuaded that bin Laden slipped away in the first 10 days of December.

MISSING THE BIG PICTURE

After-action reviews, conducted privately inside and outside the military chain of command, describe the episode as a significant defeat for the United States. A common view among those interviewed outside the U.S. Central Command is that Army Gen. Tommy R. Franks, the war's operational commander, misjudged the interests of putative Afghan allies and let pass the best chance to capture or kill al Qaeda's leader. Without professing second thoughts about Tora Bora, Franks has changed his approach fundamentally in subsequent battles, using Americans on the ground as first-line combat units.

In the fight for Tora Bora, corrupt local militias did not live up to promises to seal off the mountain redoubt [fortification], and some colluded in the escape of fleeing al Qaeda fighters. Franks did not perceive the setbacks soon enough, some officials said, because he ran the war from Tampa with no commander on the scene above the rank of lieutenant colonel. The first Americans did not arrive until three days into the fighting. "No one had the big picture," one defense official said.

The Bush administration has never acknowledged that bin Laden slipped through the cordon ostensibly placed around Tora Bora as U.S. aircraft began bombing on Nov. 30. Until now it was not known publicly whether the al Qaeda leader was present on the battlefield.

But inside the government there is little controversy on the subject. Captured al Qaeda fighters, interviewed separately, gave consistent accounts describing an address by bin Laden around Dec. 3 to *mujaheddin*, or holy warriors, dug into the warren of caves and tunnels built as a redoubt against Soviet invaders in the 1980s. One official said "we had a good piece of sigint," or signals intelligence, confirming those reports.

A LACK OF CONCRETE PROOF

"I don't think you can ever say with certainty, but we did conclude he was there, and that conclusion has strengthened with time," said another official, giving an authoritative account of the intelligence consensus. "We have high confidence that he was there, and also high confidence, but not as high, that he got out. We have several accounts of that from people who are in detention, al Qaeda people who were free at the time and are not free now."

Franks continues to dissent from that analysis. Rear Adm.
Craig Quigley, his chief spokesman, acknowledged the dominant view outside Tampa but said the general is unpersuaded.

"We have never seen anything that was convincing to us at
all that Osama bin Laden was present at any stage of Tora
Bora—before, during or after," Quigley said. "I know you've
got voices in the intelligence community that are taking a different view, but I just wanted you to know our view as well."

"Truth is hard to come by in Afghanistan," Quigley said,
and for confidence on bin Laden's whereabouts "you need to
see some sort of physical concrete proof."

THE ROLES OF AFGHANS AND PAKISTANIS

Franks has told subordinates that it was vital at the Tora
Bora battle, among the first to include allies from Afghanistan's Pashtun majority, to take a supporting role and "not
just push them aside and take over because we were America," according to Quigley.

"Our relationship with the Afghans in the south and east
was entirely different at that point in the war," he said. "It's
no secret that we had a much more mature relationship with
the Northern Alliance fighters." Franks, he added, "still
thinks that the process he followed of helping the anti-
Taliban forces around Tora Bora, to make sure it was crystal clear to them that we were not there to conquer their
country . . . was absolutely the right thing to do."

With the collapse of the Afghan cordon around Tora Bora,

and the decision to hold back U.S. troops from the Army's 10th Mountain Division, Pakistan stepped in. The government of President Pervez Musharraf moved thousands of troops to his border with Afghanistan and intercepted about 300 of the estimated 1,000 al Qaeda fighters who escaped Tora Bora. U.S. officials said close to half of the detainees now held at the U.S. base at Guantanamo Bay, Cuba, were turned over by the Pakistani government.

THEORIES ABOUT BIN LADEN

Those successes included none of the top al Qaeda leaders at Tora Bora, officials acknowledged. Of the dozen senior leaders identified by the U.S. government, two are now accounted for—Muhammad Atef, believed dead in a Hellfire missile attack, and Abu Zubaida, taken into custody late last month. But "most of the people we have been authorized to kill are still breathing," said an official directly involved in the pursuit, and several of them were at Tora Bora.

The predominant view among the analysts is that bin Laden is alive, but knowledgeable officials said they cannot rule out the possibility that he died at Tora Bora or afterward. Some analysts believe bin Laden is seriously ill and under the medical care of his second-in-command, Ayman Zawahiri, an Egyptian-trained physician. One of the theories, none supported by firm evidence, is that he has Marfan syndrome, a congenital disorder of some people with bin Laden's tall, slender body type that puts them at increased risk of heart attack or stroke.

The minority of U.S. officials who argue that bin Laden is probably dead note that four months have passed since any credible trace of him has surfaced in intelligence collection. Those who argue that he is probably alive note that monitoring of a proven network of bin Laden contacts has turned up no evidence of reaction to his death. If he had died, surely there would have been some detectable echo within this network, these officials argue.

FRUSTRATION AT MISSED OPPORTUNITIES

In public, the Bush administration acknowledges no regret about its prosecution of Tora Bora. One official spokesman, declining to be named, described questions about the battle as "navel-gazing" and said the national security team is "too busy for that." He added, "We leave that to you guys in the press."

But some policymakers and operational officers spoke in frustrated and even profane terms of what they called an opportunity missed.

"We [messed] up by not getting into Tora Bora sooner and letting the Afghans do all the work," said a senior official with direct responsibilities in counterterrorism. "Clearly a decision point came when we started bombing Tora Bora and we decided just to bomb, because that's when he escaped. . . . We didn't put U.S. forces on the ground, despite all the brave talk, and that is what we have had to change since then."

When al Qaeda forces began concentrating again in February, south of the town of Gardez, Franks moved in thousands of U.S. troops from the 101st Airborne Division and the 10th Mountain Division. In the battle of Shahikot in early March—also known as Operation Anaconda—the United States let Afghan allies attack first. But when that offensive stalled, American infantry units took it up.

PRESIDENT BUSH'S CHANGE OF FOCUS

Another change since Tora Bora, with no immediate prospect of finding bin Laden, is that President Bush has stopped proclaiming the goal of taking him "dead or alive" and now avoids previous references to the al Qaeda founder as public enemy number one.

In an interview with *The Washington Post* in late December, Bush displayed a scorecard of al Qaeda leaders on which he had drawn the letter X through the faces of those thought dead. By last month, Bush began saying that continued public focus on individual terrorists, including bin Laden, meant that "people don't understand the scope of the mission."

"Terror is bigger than one person," Bush said March 14. "He's a person that's now been marginalized." The president said bin Laden had "met his match" and "may even be dead," and added: "I truly am not that concerned about him."

Top advisers now assert that the al Qaeda leader's fate should be no measure of U.S. success in the war.

"The goal there was never after specific individuals," Gen. Richard B. Myers, chairman of the Joint Chiefs of Staff, said last week. "It was to disrupt the terrorists."

BIN LADEN'S CAPTURE A PRIME OBJECTIVE

Said Quigley at the Central Command: "There's no question that Osama bin Laden is the head of al Qaeda, and it's always a good thing to get rid of the head of an organization if your goal is to do it harm. So would we like to get bin Laden? You bet, but al Qaeda would still exist as an organization if we got him tomorrow."

At least since the 1980s, the U.S. military has made a point of avoiding open declaration of intent to capture or kill individual enemies. Such assignments cannot be carried out with confidence, and if acknowledged they increase the stature of an enemy leader who survives. After-action disclosures have made clear, nonetheless, that finding Manuel Noriega during the Panama invasion of 1989 and Saddam Hussein in the 1991 Persian Gulf War were among the top priorities of the armed forces.

The same holds true now, high-ranking officials said in interviews on condition that they not be named. "Of course bin Laden is crucial," one said.

In Britain, Armed Forces Minister Adam Ingram told BBC radio yesterday that bin Laden's capture "remains one of the prime objectives" of the war.

The Possible Impact of Bin Laden's Capture or Death

John Arquilla

Since the attacks of September 11, 2001, many Americans have yearned for Osama bin Laden's capture or death. But some observers of the war on terror warn against placing too much hope in such outcomes. Since al Qaeda is loosely organized, these critics argue, its operations might not be adversely affected if Bin Laden were captured or killed. Moreover, Bin Laden's symbolic status among his followers might even be enhanced by his martyrdom. Soon after the U.S. failure to corner Bin Laden at Tora Bora, the international relations scholar John Arquilla wrote the following commentary for the *Los Angeles Times*. Arquilla goes so far as to suggest that Bin Laden's capture or death might be a setback rather than a victory for the United States, especially if al Qaeda should wield weapons of mass destruction. Arquilla's books include *Networks and Netwars: The Future of Terror, Crime, and Militancy*, coauthored with David Ronfeldt.

The hunt is on. With the Taliban routed, the war on terror now turns to the effort to bring back Osama bin Laden—dead or alive. While it's a natural impulse to send out the posse, maybe we shouldn't try too hard. Turning the next phase of this conflict into the most expensive manhunt in history might well divert attention and needed resources from what should be the war's central aim: to defeat Al Qaeda before it mounts an attack with a weapon of mass destruction. We can't afford to waste time: The likelihood of such an attack will only grow over the coming months.

Aside from the compelling emotional reasons for wanting to go after Bin Laden, there is also the practical matter of the impact his capture or death might have on Al Qaeda. If Al Qaeda is truly dependent upon his leadership, eliminating Bin Laden might collapse the network, severing head from hands in a way that leaves Al Qaeda operatives dangling helplessly.

But from everything we know of Al Qaeda, the group is a loosely organized, widely dispersed network without a strong central "leadership node." If this is true, then getting Bin Laden may do little to impede Al Qaeda's efforts to use whatever weapons of mass destruction it might acquire. As numerous organizational studies have shown, hierarchies can be crippled by the loss of as little as 5% of their leadership, while less top-down networks can sustain more than 10 times that loss rate and keep functioning.

LEAVING BIN LADEN "OUT THERE"

If Al Qaeda is composed of semi-autonomous cells and nodes, spread around some dozens of countries worldwide, then whichever ones have been working to develop or buy poisons, bugs or nukes will presumably keep on doing what they have been doing. And should they actually succeed, there would no doubt be little more than general guidance from Bin Laden about their use. Most of the operational details would likely be left to the discretion of the various network members. In business terms, Bin Laden's role in a networked Al Qaeda would primarily be to maintain "topsight" regarding the overall course of the terror war—not to over-control his distributed nodes.

For this reason, the loss of Bin Laden, far from crippling a networked Al Qaeda, might actually make it much harder to locate the rest of his followers. What would happen if Bin Laden is just left out there—wherever "there" ultimately is? His minions will almost certainly make efforts, however furtive, to contact him from time to time—likely using either couriers or electronic means. This would increase the chances of intercepting some messages, gleaning vitally needed intelligence.

The idea of leaving Bin Laden out there should be applied to lesser members of the network as well, which could increase opportunities for connecting more of the dots of the network structure. This strategy is standard practice both in counterespionage and in organized-crime investigations. In these realms, the Mafia don, say, is often the last to be captured, because of the intelligence payoff that comes from

Would Bin Laden's Death Create Another Che Guevara?

Like John Arquilla, some international experts question the value of killing Osama bin Laden. Milt Bearden was the CIA station chief in Pakistan from 1986 to 1989. In the following excerpt from a 2004 The New York Times *article, Bearden warns of the legendary status Bin Laden might acquire in death.*

If Mr. bin Laden is, indeed, the north star, the spirit of the jihadists' movement rather than its controller, then his death will have little effect beyond establishing his immortality and spurring America's jihadist enemies to go to even greater heights to harm the United States or its friends. [al Qaeda leader] Dr. [Ayman al-] Zawahiri's end will have even less meaning.

This could be similar to the consequences of another great manhunt that took place during my early days in the Central Intelligence Agency—the hunt for Che Guevara, the north star of the 1960's communist revolutionaries in Latin America. After a wide-scale effort, Guevara was tracked down and killed in Bolivia in 1967. But his dream didn't die there. His myth continued to inspire revolutionary movements in Latin America and beyond—his death is still marked every five years in capitals throughout the world—and the myth lives on because of the circumstances of his death. It was considered a romantic, almost glamorous denouement.

Perhaps some in Washington are already speculating whether it will be better to try to capture Mr. bin Laden, knowing that his death will guarantee his immortality.

It may be that in death both Mr. bin Laden or Dr. Zawahiri can achieve more real power than they ever wielded while alive.

Milt Bearden, "The Nation: Twists of Terror; You Cut the Head, But the Body Still Moves," *The New York Times*, March 21, 2004.

monitoring communications coming his way. Simply put, if our objective is stopping the Al Qaeda network from acquiring and using weapons of mass destruction, then—much as the mind recoils—Bin Laden becomes more valuable alive and free than dead.

Bin Laden's Probable Plans

To be sure, the push to capture or kill Bin Laden will remain high. The American need for a clearly defined antagonist—

see any Hollywood film plot—coupled with intelligence as-
sessments built on a foundation of "leadership profiles,"
guarantees this. So, do the president's repeated calls for his
capture or death, which have set the bar of political expectations quite high. And, after all, there is some chance that Bin
Laden has actually been orchestrating most of Al Qaeda's actions. Even if he is—perhaps especially if he is—we should
assume that he is at least smart enough to have planned in
advance for his own capture or demise.

Because the possibility that a secret military trial and
swift execution would deny him a bully pulpit from which to
tell his side of the story, Bin Laden has most likely made
plans to guarantee that, if cornered, he will die rather than
be captured. If he has made such preparations, our overall
war aim of denying terrorists weapons of mass destruction
may already be undermined. He could easily have moved
operators and money out across a global grid, with much of
this being done even before 9/11. His "sleepers" would no
doubt also have been instructed on the general plan of campaign, with set orders about what to do in case of his death
or capture. This latter point echoes standing orders that all
U.S. missile submarine skippers have, should they lose contact with home for a specific period. In this case, an envelope
is opened, the target list is read and the attack proceeds.

Consider what little we can say with certainty that we
know about Bin Laden: He is a man who celebrates death,
and he is a meticulous planner. Putting these two facts together, can we doubt that he has thought strategically about
his own demise? The likely nature of Bin Laden's personal
last rites merit careful consideration, as they would probably consist of some sort of bloody self-immolation that killed
those closing in on him. Perhaps this would consist of high
explosives, or some kind of big, dirty bomb. Either way, a
team trying to capture him would, in effect, be trying to
defuse a living unexploded device.

An Endless Manhunt

It is also possible that Bin Laden might try something even
more clever. He could wander off by himself, say to a remote
cave, then detonate an explosive that would bury him under a
mountain of debris. This way, the manhunt would go on forever, and his legend would only grow, like a terrorist version
of 1970s skyjacker D.B. Cooper, who parachuted from a Boe-

ing 727 with $200,000 in ransom money strapped to his waist and disappeared. Meanwhile, resources expanded in the hunt for Bin Laden would take away from efforts to roll up the rest of the network, giving his distributed nodes and cells the time and chance they would need for their dark, grand enterprise —which would still be guided by his dead hand.

It is folly to believe that Bin Laden has not carefully planned his personal endgame. It is folly to believe that he would have begun this terror war with no strategic vision of how he might end it, using the ultimate weapons to achieve the ultimate victory—even after his own death. For these reasons, it may be the ultimate folly on our part to concentrate so much on capturing or killing him while the rest of Al Qaeda feverishly pursues the weapons of mass destruction that could prove the instrument of our defeat. If instead we should let him run free and beef up our worldwide efforts against Al Qaeda, we may learn enough to destroy this network before it can pose a mortal threat to us.

Osama bin Laden Resurfaces

Osama bin Laden

Four days before the 2004 U.S. presidential election, Osama bin Laden made a dramatic reappearance. On October 29, the Arabic-language television network Al Jazeera broadcast excerpts of a videotaped speech by Bin Laden. Clad in a turban, a white robe, and a gold cloak, Bin Laden appeared remarkably healthy, despite speculations that he had been injured in the bombing of Tora Bora. Al Jazeera released a complete transcript of Bin Laden's eighteen-minute message to the American people, which is reprinted here. For the first time, Bin Laden admitted his role in planning the attacks of September 11, 2001. He also criticized President George W. Bush, revealed al Qaeda's plan to bankrupt the United States, and promised the American people renewed security if they changed their policies in the Middle East.

Praise be to Allah who created the creation for his worship and commanded them to be just and permitted the wronged one to retaliate against the oppressor in kind. To proceed:

Peace be upon he who follows the guidance: People of America this talk of mine is for you and concerns the ideal way to prevent another Manhattan, and deals with the war and its causes and results.

DISTORTION AND DECEPTION

Before I begin, I say to you that security is an indispensable pillar of human life and that free men do not forfeit their security, contrary to [President] Bush's claim that we hate freedom.

If so, then let him explain to us why we don't strike for example—Sweden? And we know that freedom-haters don't

Osama bin Laden, "Full Transcript of Bin Laden's Speech," www.aljazeera.net, November 1, 2004.

possess defiant spirits like those of the 19 [al Qaeda operatives who hijacked the planes on September 11, 2001]—may Allah have mercy on them.

No, we fight because we are free men who don't sleep under oppression. We want to restore freedom to our nation, just as you lay waste to our nation. So shall we lay waste to yours.

No one except a dumb thief plays with the security of others and then makes himself believe he will be secure. Whereas thinking people, when disaster strikes, make it their priority to look for its causes, in order to prevent it happening again.

But I am amazed at you. Even though we are in the fourth year after the events of September 11th, Bush is still engaged in distortion, deception and hiding from you the real causes. And thus, the reasons are still there for a repeat of what occurred.

So I shall talk to you about the story behind those events and shall tell you truthfully about the moments in which the decision was taken, for you to consider.

THE CROCODILE AND THE CHILD

I say to you, Allah knows that it had never occurred to us to strike the towers [of the World Trade Center]. But after it became unbearable and we witnessed the oppression and tyranny of the American/Israeli coalition against our people in Palestine and Lebanon, it came to my mind.

The events that affected my soul in a direct way started in 1982 when America permitted the Israelis to invade Lebanon and the American Sixth Fleet helped them in that. This bombardment began and many were killed and injured and others were terrorised and displaced.

I couldn't forget those moving scenes, blood and severed limbs, women and children sprawled everywhere. Houses destroyed along with their occupants and high rises demolished over their residents, rockets raining down on our home without mercy.

The situation was like a crocodile meeting a helpless child, powerless except for his screams. Does the crocodile understand a conversation that doesn't include a weapon? And the whole world saw and heard but it didn't respond.

In those difficult moments many hard-to-describe ideas bubbled in my soul, but in the end they produced an intense feeling of rejection of tyranny, and gave birth to a strong resolve to punish the oppressors.

And as I looked at those demolished towers in Lebanon, it entered my mind that we should punish the oppressor in kind and that we should destroy towers in America in order that they taste some of what we tasted and so that they be deterred from killing our women and children.

And that day, it was confirmed to me that oppression and the intentional killing of innocent women and children is a deliberate American policy. Destruction is freedom and democracy, while resistance is terrorism and intolerance.

BIN LADEN'S MESSAGE

This means the oppressing and embargoing to death of millions as Bush Sr. did in Iraq in the greatest mass slaughter of children mankind has ever known [because of U.N. sanctions in the 1991 Gulf War], and it means the throwing of millions of pounds of bombs and explosives at millions of children—also in Iraq—as Bush Jr. did, in order to remove an old agent and replace him with a new puppet to assist in the pilfering of Iraq's oil and other outrages.

So with these images and their like as their background, the events of September 11th came as a reply to those great wrongs, should a man be blamed for defending his sanctuary?

Is defending oneself and punishing the aggressor in kind, objectionable terrorism? If it is such, then it is unavoidable for us.

This is the message which I sought to communicate to you in word and deed, repeatedly, for years before September 11th.

And you can read this, if you wish, in my interview with Scott [MacLeod] in *Time* magazine in 1996, or with Peter Arnett on CNN in 1997, or my meeting with John Weiner [contributing editor of *The Nation*] in 1998.

You can observe it practically, if you wish, in Kenya and Tanzania [where U.S. embassies were bombed] and in Aden [Yemen, where the USS *Cole* was bombed]. And you can read it in my interview with Abdul Bari Atwan [editor of *Al-Quds al-Arabi*], as well as my interviews with [British journalist] Robert Fisk.

The latter is one of your compatriots and co-religionists and I consider him to be neutral. So are the pretenders of freedom at the White House and the channels controlled by them able to run an interview with him? So that he may relay to the American people what he has understood from us to be the reasons for our fight against you?

PRIDE, ARROGANCE, AND GREED

If you were to avoid these reasons, you will have taken the correct path that will lead America to the security that it was in before September 11th. This concerned the causes of the war.

As for its results, they have been, by the grace of Allah, positive and enormous, and have, by all standards, exceeded all expectations. This is due to many factors, chief among them, that we have found it difficult to deal with the Bush administration in light of the resemblance it bears to the regimes in our countries, half of which are ruled by the military and the other half which are ruled by the sons of kings and presidents.

Our experience with them is lengthy, and both types are replete with those who are characterised by pride, arrogance, greed and misappropriation of wealth. This resemblance began after the visits of Bush Sr. to the region.

At a time when some of our compatriots were dazzled by America and hoping that these visits would have an effect on our countries, all of a sudden he was affected by those monarchies and military regimes, and became envious of their remaining decades in their positions, to embezzle the public wealth of the nation without supervision or accounting.

So he took dictatorship and suppression of freedoms to his son and they named it the Patriot Act, under the pretence of fighting terrorism. In addition, Bush sanctioned the installing of sons as state governors, and didn't forget to import expertise in election fraud from the region's presidents to Florida to be made use of in moments of difficulty [a reference to the disputed Florida vote during the 2000 U.S. presidential election].

All that we have mentioned has made it easy for us to provoke and bait this administration. All that we have to do is to send two mujahidin to the furthest point east to raise a piece of cloth on which is written al-Qaida, in order to make the generals race there to cause America to suffer human, economic, and political losses without their achieving for it anything of note other than some benefits for their private companies.

BANKRUPTING AMERICA

This is in addition to our having experience in using guerrilla warfare and the war of attrition to fight tyrannical superpowers, as we, alongside the mujahidin, bled Russia for 10 years, until it went bankrupt and was forced to withdraw in defeat.

All Praise is due to Allah.

So we are continuing this policy in bleeding America to the point of bankruptcy. Allah willing, and nothing is too great for Allah.

That being said, those who say that al-Qaida has won against the administration in the White House or that the administration has lost in this war have not been precise, because when one scrutinises the results, one cannot say that al-Qaida is the sole factor in achieving those spectacular gains.

"BIN LADEN IS CAPTURED" RUMORS AND THE STOCK MARKET

In his videotaped speech of October 2004, Osama bin Laden threatened to bankrupt the United States. In fact, the war against Bin Laden affects America's financial institutions in startling ways. In the following excerpt from an item posted on Snopes.com, Internet writer Barbara Mikkelson describes how rumors of Bin Laden's capture have affected the stock market.

"Osama captured" whispers have been churning in the rumor mill since scant weeks after the September 11 attacks. For the past couple of years, flagging financial markets have rallied on such chatter, turning downtrends into upswings. On 22 May 2002, a two-day selling spree was momentarily reversed, sending the Dow and the NASDAQ to seasonal highs, after rumors that Osama bin Laden had been captured swept the trading floor. Within 55 minutes, the Dow shot up over 100 points. Likewise, falling prices on the New York Stock Exchange were given a temporary shot in the arm on 20 August 2003 by a rumor that United States forces had captured Osama bin Laden. Yet in terms of market rally, the most effective "we got him!" rumor was the first, which occurred on 11 October 2001. On the strength of that rumor, giddy investors helped push major stock indexes close to levels not seen since the September 11 attacks, lifting the Dow by 167 points and the NASDAQ by 75.

Barbara Mikkelson, "Osama bin Laden Captured?" Snopes.com, 2004. www.snopes.com.

Rather, the policy of the White House that demands the opening of war fronts to keep busy their various corporations—whether they be working in the field of arms or oil or reconstruction—has helped al-Qaida to achieve these enormous results.

And so it has appeared to some analysts and diplomats that the White House and us are playing as one team towards the economic goals of the United States, even if the intentions differ.

THE COST TO AMERICA

And it was to these sorts of notions and their like that the British diplomat and others were referring in their lectures at the Royal Institute of International Affairs [in London]. [When they pointed out that] for example, al-Qaida spent $500,000 on the event, while America, in the incident and its aftermath, lost—according to the lowest estimate—more than $500 billion.

Meaning that every dollar of al-Qaida defeated a million dollars by the permission of Allah, besides the loss of a huge number of jobs.

As for the size of the economic deficit, it has reached record astronomical numbers estimated to total more than a trillion dollars.

And even more dangerous and bitter for America is that the mujahidin recently forced Bush to resort to emergency funds to continue the fight in Afghanistan and Iraq, which is evidence of the success of the bleed-until-bankruptcy plan —with Allah's permission.

It is true that this shows that al-Qaida has gained, but on the other hand, it shows that the Bush administration has also gained, something of which anyone who looks at the size of the contracts acquired by the shady Bush administration-linked mega-corporations, like Halliburton [a defense contractor] and its kind, will be convinced. And it all shows that the real loser is . . . you.

BUSH'S BLURRED VISION

It is the American people and their economy. And for the record, we had agreed with the Commander-General Muhammad Ataa [leader of the September 11 attacks], Allah have mercy on him, that all the operations should be carried out within 20 minutes, before Bush and his administration notice.

It never occurred to us that the commander-in-chief of the American armed forces would abandon 50,000 of his citizens in the twin towers to face those great horrors alone, the time when they most needed him.

But because it seemed to him that occupying himself by talking to the little girl about the goat and its butting [while reading with schoolchildren in Florida] was more important than occupying himself with the planes and their butting of the skyscrapers, we were given three times the period required to execute the operations—all praise is due to Allah.

And it's no secret to you that the thinkers and perceptive ones from among the Americans warned Bush before the war and told him: "All that you want for securing America and removing the weapons of mass destruction—assuming they exist—is available to you, and the nations of the world are with you in the inspections, and it is in the interest of America that it not be thrust into an unjustified war with an unknown outcome."

But the darkness of the black gold blurred his vision and insight, and he gave priority to private interests over the public interests of America.

So the war went ahead, the death toll rose, the American economy bled, and Bush became embroiled in the swamps of Iraq that threaten his future. He fits the saying "like the naughty she-goat who used her hoof to dig up a knife from under the earth."

GESTURES OF DESPAIR

So I say to you, over 15,000 of our people have been killed and tens of thousands injured, while more than a thousand of you have been killed and more than 10,000 injured. And Bush's hands are stained with the blood of all those killed from both sides, all for the sake of oil and keeping their private companies in business.

Be aware that it is the nation who punishes the weak man when he causes the killing of one of its citizens for money, while letting the powerful one get off, when he causes the killing of more than 1000 of its sons, also for money.

And the same goes for your allies in Palestine. They terrorise the women and children, and kill and capture the men as they lie sleeping with their families on the mattresses, that you may recall that for every action, there is a reaction.

Finally, it behoves you to reflect on the last wills and testaments of the thousands who left you on the 11th as they gestured in despair. They are important testaments, which should be studied and researched.

Among the most important of what I read in them was some prose in their gestures before the collapse, where they say: "How mistaken we were to have allowed the White House to implement its aggressive foreign policies against the weak without supervision."

It is as if they were telling you, the people of America: "Hold to account those who have caused us to be killed, and happy is he who learns from others' mistakes."

And among that which I read in their gestures is a verse of poetry. "Injustice chases its people, and how unhealthy the bed of tyranny."

THE GUARANTEE OF AMERICAN SECURITY

As has been said: "An ounce of prevention is better than a pound of cure."

And know that: "It is better to return to the truth than persist in error." And that the wise man doesn't squander his security, wealth and children for the sake of the liar in the White House.

In conclusion, I tell you in truth, that your security is not in the hands of Kerry, nor Bush, nor al-Qaida. No.

Your security is in your own hands. And every state that doesn't play with our security has automatically guaranteed its own security.

And Allah is our Guardian and Helper, while you have no Guardian or Helper. All peace be upon he who follows the Guidance.

APPENDIX OF DOCUMENTS

DOCUMENT 1: ISLAMIC SCHOLAR IBN TAYMIYAH ARGUES THAT THE "GREATER GOOD" MUST PREVAIL IN *JIHAD*

One of Osama bin Laden's intellectual heroes is the medieval Islamic theologian and jurist Taqial-din ibn Taymiyah (1263–1328). Bin Laden has been noticeably influenced by Ibn Taymiyah's arguments concerning how evil actions are sometimes needed to achieve a greater good. For example, in the following excerpts from his writings, Ibn Taymiyah claims that even killing innocent civilians may be necessary during jihad.

Since it is proved that good things lead to benefits, leaving them undone is considered as an evil, and evils are harmful. An undesirable thing may also involve some benefits. Conflict happens between two good things that cannot be combined together, and so the better one should be taken; between two bad things that cannot be averted, so the lesser of them has to be accepted; or between a good thing and a bad thing which have to be taken together or left together, and so should be taken or left according to which is bigger: the benefit involved in the good thing or the evil inhering the bad thing. . . .

Also in the fiqh [understanding] of jihad, while killing noncombatant women and children and their like is harem [forbidden], they may be killed if need arises for a type of combat that includes them, such as using mangonels [large, medieval siege weapons that hurl boulders] or night raids, as is narrated in the Sunna [sayings and deeds of Mohammed] with regard to striking a siege around Taif and launching stones on it with the mangonel, and also with regard to raiding infidels, who are residing in the Muslim country, by night. This judgment is also aimed at averting the occurrence of fitna (temptation against one's creed) by killing those who, otherwise, should not be killed intentionally.

And such is the issue of tatarrus [the use of innocent people as human shields], mentioned by faqihs (jurists). Jihad is a fight against the dissent sown by unbelief, which is fought even if this involves accepting lesser evils. Therefore, faqihs agree that when the evil against Muslims can only be averted by means leading to killing those human shields. then they may be killed in some opinions. . . .

If two duties coincide but only one can be done and the more important is chosen, then the other is no longer a duty, and he who leaves it for the more important duty will not be shirking a duty.

Similarly, if two prohibited things combine so that the lesser of them has to be committed in order to avert the larger one, doing the lesser one will not be prohibited in fact. . . . It is said in this connection, "The duty was left for an excuse and the evil was done for the sake of preponderant interest, or for the sake of necessity, or for averting a worse evil."

Taqial-din ibn Taymiyah, fatwa, Yusuf al-Qaradawi, *Priorities of the Islamic Movement in the Coming Phase.* Witness-Pioneer: A Virtual Islamic Organization. www. witness-pioneer.org.

DOCUMENT 2: ISLAMIC INTELLECTUAL SAYYID QUTB ASSERTS THAT "ISLAM IS THE REAL CIVILIZATION"

Sayyid Qutb (1906–1966) is often called the intellectual founder of today's Islamist movement. His 1964 book Milestones *(also known as* Signposts Along the Road*) had a profound influence on Osama bin Laden, who was a university student of Qutb's brother Muhammad. Central to Sayyid Qutb's thinking is the Islamic concept of* jahiliyya, *or ignorance of the ways of God. Qutb called for universal jihad (struggle) against* jahiliyya, *especially the corrupting influences of the West. Bin Laden's contempt for the decadence of Western culture is strongly reflected in the following excerpts from* Milestones.

Indeed, Islam establishes the values and morals which are "human"—those which develop characteristics in a human being which distinguish him from the animals. In whatever society Islam is dominant, whether it is an agricultural or industrial society, nomadic and pastoral or urban and settled, poor or rich, it implants these human values and morals, nurtures them and strengthens them; it develops human characteristics progressively and guards against degeneration toward animalism. The direction of the line which separates human values from animal-like characteristics is upward; but if this direction is reversed, then in spite of all material progress the civilization will be "backward", "degenerative", and "jahili"!

If the family is the basis of the society, and the basis of the family is the division of labor between husband and wife, and the upbringing of children is the most important function of the family, then such a society is indeed civilized. In the Islamic system of life, this kind of a family provides the environment under which human values and morals develop and grow in the new generation; these values and morals cannot exist apart from the family unit. If, on the other hand, free sexual relationships and illegitimate children become the basis of a society, and if the relationship between man and woman is based on lust, passion and impulse, and the division of work is not based on family responsibility and natural gifts; if woman's role is merely to be attractive, sexy and flirtatious, and if woman is freed from her basic responsibility of bringing up children; and if, on her own or under social demand, she prefers to become a hostess or a stewardess in a hotel or ship or air company, thus spending her ability for material productivity rather than in the training of human beings, because material production is considered to be more important, more valuable and more honorable than the development of human character, then such a civilization is "backward" from the human point of view, or "jahili" in the Islamic terminology.

The family system and the relationship between the sexes determine the whole character of a society and whether it is backward or civilized, jahili or Islamic. Those societies which give ascendance to physical desires and animalistic morals cannot be considered civilized, no matter how much progress they may make in industry or science. This is the only measure which does not err in gauging true human progress.

In all modern jahili societies, the meaning of "morality" is limited to such an extent that all those aspects which distinguish man from animal are considered beyond its sphere. In these societies, illegitimate sexual relationships, even homosexuality, are not considered immoral. The meaning of ethics is limited to economic affairs or sometimes to political affairs which fall into the category of "government interests."...

Among jahili societies, writers, journalists and editors advise both married and unmarried people that free sexual relationships are not immoral. However, it is immoral if a boy uses his partner, or a girl uses her partner, for sex, while feeling no love in his or her heart. It is bad if a wife continues to guard her chastity while her love for her husband has vanished; it is admirable if she finds another lover. Dozens of stories are written about this theme; many newspaper editorials, articles, cartoons, serious and light columns all invite to this way of life.

From the point of view of "human" progress, all such societies are not civilized but are backward.

The line of human progress goes upward from animal desires toward higher values. To control the animal desires, a progressive society lays down the foundation of a family system in which human desires find satisfaction, as well as providing for the future generation to be brought up in such a manner that it will continue the human civilization, in which human characteristics flower to their full bloom. Obviously a society which intends to control the animal characteristics, while providing full opportunities for the development and perfection of human characteristics, requires strong safeguards for the peace and stability of the family, so that it may perform its basic task free from the influences of impulsive passions. On the other hand, if in a society immoral teachings and poisonous suggestions are rampant, and sexual activity is consid-

ered outside the sphere of morality, then in that society the humanity of man can hardly find a place to develop.

Thus, only Islamic values and morals, Islamic teachings and safeguards, are worthy of mankind, and from this unchanging and true
measure of human progress, Islam is the real civilization and Islamic society is truly civilized.

Sayyid Qutb, *Milestones*. 1964. Young Muslims Inc. www.youngmuslims.ca.

DOCUMENT 3: PALESTINIAN SCHOLAR ABDULLAH AZZAM ENCOURAGES MUSLIMS TO TAKE PART IN THE AFGHAN JIHAD

*The Palestinian scholar Abdullah Azzam had a profound impact on
today's radical Islamic movement. Osama bin Laden was a student
at King Abdul Aziz University in Jeddah, Saudi Arabia, when Azzam was a professor there. Azzam became Bin Laden's mentor when
they both served in the Soviet-Afghan War during the 1980s. In writings like the following excerpt from* Join the Caravan, *Azzam inspired Bin Laden and many other Muslims to take part in the
Afghan jihad.*

Praise be to Allah, Lord of the Worlds. Blessings and peace be upon
the noblest of Messengers, Muhammad, and upon all his family
and companions.

1. We have spoken at length about the status of jihad today in Afghanistan, Palestine, and other usurped Muslim lands of the like.
We have confirmed what has been agreed upon by the earlier
(salaf) and latter (khalaf) generations of hadith [collections of Mohammed's sayings and deeds] scholars, exegetes, jurists, and scholars of religious principles (usul), namely that: "When a span of
Muslim land is occupied jihad becomes individually obligatory
(fard'ayn) on the inhabitants of that piece of land. The woman may
go out [to take part in jihad] without her husband's permission
with a mahram [close male relative], the one in debt without the
permission of the one to whom he owes, the child without his father's permission. If the inhabitants of that area are not sufficient
in number, fall short, or are lazy, the individually obligatory nature
of jihad extends to those around them, and so on and so on until it
covers the entire Earth, being individually obligatory (fard'ayn)
just like salah, fasting, and the like so that nobody may abandon it."

2. The obligation of jihad today remains fard'ayn until the liberation of the last piece of land which was in the hands of Muslims
but has been occupied by the Disbelievers.

3. Some scholars consider jihad today in Afghanistan and Palestine to be fard kifayah [not obligatory to all Muslims]. We agree with
them in that jihad in Afghanistan for the Arabs was initially fard kifayah. But the jihad is in need of men and the inhabitants of Afghanistan have not met the requirement which is to expel the Disbelievers from Afghanistan. In this case, the communal obligation (fard

kifayah) is overturned. It becomes individually obligatory (fard'ayn) in Afghanistan, and remains so until enough Mujahideen [holy warriors] have gathered to expel the communists in which case it again becomes fard kifayah.

4. There is no permission needed from anybody in the case of an individual obligation (fard'ayn), according to the principle, "there is no permission necessary for an individual obligation (fard'ayn)".

5. A person who discourages people from jihad is like the one who discourages people from fasting. Whoever advises an able Muslim not to go for jihad is just like the one who advises him to eat in [the holy month of] Ramadan while he is healthy and in residence.

6. It is best to shun the company of those who hold back from jihad and not to enter into arguments with them, for this would lead to idle disputation and hardening of the heart. Shaykh al-Islam Ibn Taymiyyah says, "And avoidance comprises: avoiding evil and evil people, and similarly shunning those who call for innovation in religion, and sinful people and those who associate with such people or assist them in those endeavours. Similar is the case of the person who abandons jihad and from whom there is no benefit in associating with, for in this case we are liable to punishment for not having helped him by co-operating in matters of righteousness and piety.

"The adulterers, homosexuals, those who abandon jihad, the innovators and the alcoholics, as well as those who associate with them are a source of harm to the religion of Islam. They will not co-operate in matters of righteousness and piety. So whoever does not shun their company is, in fact, abandoning what he has been commanded to do and is committing a despicable deed."

Imam Abdullah Azzam, *Join the Caravan*. Religioscope. www.religioscope.com.

DOCUMENT 4: OSAMA BIN LADEN REMEMBERS THE AFGHAN JIHAD

Osama bin Laden's participation in the Soviet-Afghan War of 1979–1989 was surely among the key experiences of his life. In 1997, CNN reporter Peter Arnett went to Afghanistan to interview Bin Laden. In the following excerpt from the interview, Bin Laden recalled the Afghan jihad and talked about the impact it had upon the Islamist movement.

Arnett: Mr. Bin Ladin, tell us about your experience during the Afghan war and what did you do during that jihad?

BIN LADIN: Praise be to God, the Cherisher and Sustainer of the worlds, that He made it possible for us to aid the Mujahidin [holy warriors] in Afghanistan without any declaration for jihad. It was rather the news that was broadcast by radio stations that the Soviet Union invaded a Muslim country. This was a sufficient motivation for me to start to aid our brothers in Afghanistan. I have benefited so greatly from the jihad in Afghanistan that it would have been impossible for me to gain such a benefit from any other chance and this cannot be measured by tens of years but rather more than that, Praise and Gratitude be to God. In spite of the Soviet power, we used to move with confidence and God conferred favors on us so that we transported heavy equipment from the country of the Two Holy Places (Arabia) estimated at hundreds of tons altogether that included bulldozers, loaders, dump trucks and equipment for digging trenches. When we saw the brutality of the Russians bombing Mujahidins' positions, by the grace of God, we dug a good number of huge tunnels and built in them some storage places and in some others we built a hospital. We also dug some roads, by the grace of God, Praise and glory be to Him, one of which you came by to us tonight. So our experience in this jihad was great, by the grace of God, Praise and Glory be to Him, and the most of what we benefited from was that the myth of the super power was destroyed not only in my mind but also in the minds of all Muslims. Slumber and fatigue vanished and so was the terror which the US would use in its media by attributing itself super power status or which the Soviet Union used by attributing itself as a super power. Today, the entire Muslim world, by the grace of God, has imbibed the faithful spirit of strength and started to interact in a good manner in order to bring an end to occupation and the Western and American influence on our countries.

Arnett: Mr. Bin Ladin, what was the significance of the Afghan war for the Islamic movement? Veterans of that war are fighting for Islamic movements and conflicts from the former Soviet republics such as Chechnya to Bosnia to Algeria. Can you explain that phenomenon to us?

BIN LADIN: As I mentioned in my answer to the previous question, the effect of jihad has been great not only at the level of the Islamic movement but rather at the level of the Muslim nation in the whole world. The spirit of power, dignity and confidence has grown in our sons and brothers for this religion and the power of God, Praise and Glory be to Him. And it has become apparent even to the Islamic movement that there is no choice but [to] return to the original spring, to this religion, to God's Book, Praise and Glory be to Him, and to the sunna [sayings and deeds] of His Prophet, Peace be upon him, as understood by our predecessors, may God be pleased with them. Of this, the acme of this religion is jihad. The nation has had a strong conviction that there is no way to obtain faithful strength but by returning to this jihad. The influence of the Afghan jihad on the Islamic world was so great and it necessitates that people should rise above many of their differences and unite their efforts against their enemy. Today, the nation is interacting well by uniting its efforts through jihad against the US which has in collaboration with the Israeli government led the ferocious campaign against the Islamic World in occupying the holy sites of the Muslims. As for the young men who participated in jihad here, their number, by the grace of God, was quite big, Praise and Gratitude be to Him, and they spread in every place in which non-believers' injustice is perpetuated against Muslims. Their going to Bosnia, Chechnya, Tajikistan and other countries is but a fulfill-ment of a duty, because we believe that these states are part of the Islamic World. Therefore, any act of aggression against any of this land of a span of hand measure makes it a duty for Muslims to send a sufficient number of their sons to fight off that aggression.

Peter Arnett, interview with Osama bin Laden, March 1997. FindLaw.com. http://news.findlaw.com.

DOCUMENT 5: BIN LADEN RECOUNTS THE FAILURES OF THE SAUDI REGIME

Osama bin Laden issued his first fatwa (religious decree) in 1996. Entitled "Declaration of War Against the Americans Occupying the Land of the Two Holy Places," this document reserves some of its harshest criticism for the rulers of Saudi Arabia. In the following excerpt, Bin Laden especially condemns the Saudi regime for allowing Americans to occupy and exploit the region.

People are fully concerned about their everyday livings; everybody talks about the deterioration of the economy, inflation, ever in-creasing debts and jails full of prisoners. Government employees with limited income talk about debts of ten thousands and hundred thousands of Saudi Riyals [unit of currency]. They complain that the value of the Riyal is greatly and continuously deteriorating among most of the main currencies. Great merchants and contrac-tors speak about hundreds and thousands of million Riyals owed to them by the government. More than three hundred forty billions of Riyals owed by the government to the people in addition to the daily accumulated interest, let alone the foreign debt. People won-der whether we are the largest oil exporting country?! They even believe that this situation is a curse put on them by Allah for not ob-jecting to the oppressive and illegitimate behaviour and measures of the ruling regime: Ignoring the divine Shari'ah [religiously in-spired] law; depriving people of their legitimate rights; allowing the American[s] to occupy the land of the two Holy Places; impris-onment, unjustly, of the sincere scholars. The honourable Ulamah [people learned in Islam] and scholars as well as merchants, econ-omists and eminent people of the country were all alerted by this disastrous situation.

Quick efforts were made by each group to contain and to correct the situation. All agreed that the country is heading toward a great catastrophe, the depth of which is not known except by Allah. One big merchant commented: "the king is leading the state into 'sixty-six' fold disaster". (We bemoan this and can only say: "No power and power acquiring except through Allah"). Numerous princes share with the people their feelings, privately expressing their concerns and objecting to the corruption, repression and the intimidation taking place in the country. But the competition between influential princes for personal gains and interest has destroyed the country. Through its course of actions the regime has torn off its legitimacy:

(1) Suspension of the Islamic Shari'ah law and exchanging it with manmade civil law. The regime entered into a bloody confrontation with the truthful Ulamah and the righteous youths (we sanctify nobody; Allah sanctify Whom He pleaseth).

(2) The inability of the regime to protect the country, and allowing the enemy of the Ummah [Islamic community]—the American crusader forces—to occupy the land for the longest of years. The crusader forces became the main cause of our disastrous condition, particularly in the economical aspect of it due to the unjustified heavy spending on these forces. As a result of the policy imposed on the country, especially in the field of oil industry where production is restricted or expanded and prices are fixed to suit the American economy ignoring the economy of the country. Expensive deals were imposed on the country to purchase arms. People [are] asking what is the justification for the very existence of the regime then?

Quick efforts were made by individuals and by different groups of the society to contain the situation and to prevent the danger. They advised the government both privately and openly; they sen[t] letters and poems, reports after reports, reminders after reminders; they explored every avenue and enlist[ed] every influential man in their movement of reform and correction. They wrote with style of passion, diplomacy and wisdom asking for corrective measures and repentance from the "great wrong doings and corruption" that had engulfed even the basic principles of the religion and the legitimate rights of the people.

But—to our deepest regret—the regime refused to listen to the people accusing them of being ridiculous and imbecile. The matter got worse as previous wrong doings were followed by mischiefs of greater magnitudes. All of this taking place in the land of the two Holy Places! It is no longer possible to be quiet. It is not acceptable to give a blind eye to this matter.

Osama bin Laden, "Ladenese Epistle: Declaration of War," 1996. www.washington post.com.

DOCUMENT 6: BIN LADEN EXTOLS MARTYRDOM

In his fatwa of 1996, Osama bin Laden promises young Muslims a glorious martyrdom if they die fighting the infidels. He also makes many references to Islamic history and sacred literature. For example, in the following excerpt, he reminds his readers of a well-known story about the angel Gabriel and the Prophet Mohammed.

I remind the youths of the Islamic world, who fought in Afghanistan and Bosnia-Herzegovina with their wealth, pens, tongues and themselves that the battle ha[s] not finished yet. I remind them about the talk between Jibreel (Gabriel) and the messenger of Allah (Allah's Blessings and Salutations may be on both of them) after the battle of Ahzab when the messenger of Allah (Allah's Blessings and Salutations may be on him) returned to Medina and before putting his sword aside; when Jibreel (Allah's Blessings and Salutations may be on him) descend[ed] saying: "[A]re you putting your sword aside? [B]y Allah the angels haven't dropped their arms yet; march with your companions to Bani Quraydah, I am (going) ahead of you to throw fears in their hearts and to shake their fortresses on them". Jibreel marched with the angels (Allah's Blessings and Salutations may be on them all), followed by the messenger of Allah (Allah's Blessings and Salutations may be on him). . . .

These youths know that: if one is not to be killed one will die (anyway) and the most honourable death is to be killed in the way of Allah. They are even more determined after the martyrdom of the four heroes who bombed the Americans in Riyadh [Saudi Arabia]. Those youths who raised high the head of the Ummah [Islamic community] and humiliated the Americans—the occupier—by their operation in Riyadh. They remember the poetry of Ja'far, the second commander in the battle of Mu'tah [629 c.e.], in which three thousand Muslims faced over a hundred thousand Romans:

> How good is the Paradise and its nearness, good with cool drink. But the Romans are promised punishment (in Hell), if I meet them.
>
> I will fight them.

And the poetry of Abdullah Bin Rawaha, the third commander in the battle of Mu'tah, after the martyrdom of Ja'far, when he felt some hesitation:

> O my soul if you do not get killed, you are going to die, anyway.
>
> This is death pool in front of you!

You are getting what you have wished for (martyrdom) before, and you follow the example of the two previous commanders[;] you are rightly guided!

Osama bin Laden, "Ladenese Epistle: Declaration of War," 1996. www.washingtonpost.com.

DOCUMENT 7: BIN LADEN'S CALL FOR JIHAD AGAINST AMERICA

Osama bin Laden's second fatwa, issued on February 23, 1998, had a special impact because it heralded the founding of the World Islamic Front for Fighting Jews and Christians, an organization of Muslim militants that extended beyond al Qaeda. In the 1998 fatwa, excerpted here, Bin Laden and his cosigners call upon Muslims worldwide to kill Americans and their allies.

The Arabian Peninsula has never—since God made it flat, created its desert, and encircled it with seas—been stormed by any forces like the crusader armies spreading in it like locusts, eating its riches and wiping out its plantations. All this is happening at a time in which nations are attacking Muslims like people fighting over a plate of food. In the light of the grave situation and the lack of support, we and you are obliged to discuss current events, and we should all agree on how to settle the matter.

No one argues today about three facts that are known to everyone; we will list them, in order to remind everyone:

First, for over seven years the United States has been occupying the lands of Islam in the holiest of places, the Arabian Peninsula, plundering its riches, dictating to its rulers, humiliating its people, terrorizing its neighbors, and turning its bases in the Peninsula into a spearhead through which to fight the neighboring Muslim peoples.

If some people have in the past argued about the fact of the occupation, all the people of the Peninsula have now acknowledged it. The best proof of this is the Americans' continuing aggression against the Iraqi people [after the 1991 Gulf War against Iraq] using the Peninsula as a staging post, even though all its rulers are against their territories being used to that end, but they are helpless.

Second, despite the great devastation inflicted on the Iraqi people by the crusader-Zionist alliance, and despite the huge number of those killed [because of UN sanctions], which has exceeded 1 million . . . despite all this, the Americans are once again trying to repeat the horrific massacres, as though they are not content with the protracted blockade imposed after the ferocious war or the fragmentation and devastation.

So here they come to annihilate what is left of this people and to humiliate their Muslim neighbors. Third, if the Americans' aims behind these wars are religious and economic, the aim is also to serve the Jews' petty state and divert attention from its occupation of Jerusalem and murder of Muslims there. The best proof of this is their eagerness to destroy Iraq, the strongest neighboring Arab state, and their endeavor to fragment all the states of the region such as Iraq, Saudi Arabia, Egypt, and Sudan into paper statelets and through their disunion and weakness to guarantee Israel's survival and the continuation of the brutal crusade occupation of the Peninsula. . . .

On that basis, and in compliance with God's order, we issue the following fatwa to all Muslims:

The ruling to kill the Americans and their allies—civilians and military—is an individual duty for every Muslim who can do it in any country in which it is possible to do it, in order to liberate the al-Aqsa Mosque [in Jerusalem] and the holy mosque [in Mecca] from their grip, and in order for their armies to move out of all the lands of Islam, defeated and unable to threaten any Muslim. This is in accordance with the words of Almighty God, "and fight the pagans all together as they fight you all together," and "fight them until there is no more tumult or oppression, and there prevail justice and faith in God."

This is in addition to the words of Almighty God: "And why should ye not fight in the cause of God and of those who, being weak, are ill-treated (and oppressed)?—women and children, whose cry is: 'Our Lord, rescue us from this town, whose people are oppressors; and raise for us from thee one who will help!'"

We—with God's help—call on every Muslim who believes in God and wishes to be rewarded to comply with God's order to kill the Americans and plunder their money wherever and whenever they find it. We also call on Muslim ulema [legal scholars], leaders, youths, and soldiers to launch the raid on Satan's U.S. troops and the devil's supporters allying with them, and to displace those who are behind them so that they may learn a lesson.

Almighty God said: "O ye who believe, give your response to God and His Apostle, when He calleth you to that which will give you life. And know that God cometh between a man and his heart, and that it is He to whom ye shall all be gathered."

Almighty God also says: "O ye who believe, what is the matter with you, that when ye are asked to go forth in the cause of God, ye cling so heavily to the earth! Do ye prefer the life of this world to the hereafter? But little is the comfort of this life, as compared with the hereafter. Unless ye go forth, He will punish you with a grievous penalty, and put others in your place; but Him ye would not harm in the least. For God hath power over all things."

Almighty God also says: "So lose no heart, nor fall into despair. For ye must gain mastery if ye are true in faith."

Osama bin Laden, "Jihad Against Jews and Crusaders," February 23, 1998. www.washingtonpost.com.

DOCUMENT 8: PRESIDENT CLINTON ANNOUNCES ATTACKS

On August 7, 1998, Osama bin Laden and al Qaeda orchestrated two nearly simultaneous attacks on the United States embassies in Tanzania and Kenya. On August 20, President Bill Clinton made a televised speech, excerpted below, announcing that U.S. warships had launched missile strikes against Afghanistan and Sudan in retaliation. Missiles that destroyed a guerrilla training camp in Afghanistan killed no al Qaeda leaders. No evidence ever proved that the alleged chemical weapons plant destroyed in the strike against Sudan was anything more than a pharmaceutical factory.

Good afternoon.

Today I ordered our armed forces to strike at terrorist-related facilities in Afghanistan and Sudan because of the imminent threat they presented to our national security. I want to speak with you about the objective of this action and why it was necessary.

Our target was terror. Our mission was clear: to strike at the network of radical groups affiliated with and funded by Osama bin Ladin, perhaps the preeminent organizer and financier of international terrorism in the world today.

The groups associated with him come from diverse places but share a hatred for democracy, a fanatical glorification of violence, and a horrible distortion of their religion, to justify the murder of innocents. They have made the United States their adversary precisely because of what we stand for and what we stand against.

A few months ago and again this week, bin Ladin publicly vowed to wage a terrorist war against America, saying—and I quote—"We do not differentiate between those dressed in military uniforms and civilians. They're all targets."

Their mission is murder, and their history is bloody. . . .

The most recent terrorist events are fresh in our memory. Two weeks ago, 12 Americans and nearly 300 Kenyans and Tanzanians lost their lives and another 5,000 were wounded when our embassies in Nairobi and Dar es Salaam were bombed. There is convincing information from our intelligence community that the bin Ladin terrorist network was responsible for these bombings. Based on this information, we have high confidence that these bombings were planned, financed, and carried out by the organization bin Ladin leads. . . .

With compelling evidence that the bin Ladin network of terrorist groups was planning to mount further attacks against Americans and other freedom-loving people, I decided America must act. And so this morning, based on the unanimous recommendation of my national security team, I ordered our Armed Forces to take action to counter an immediate threat from the bin Ladin network.

Earlier today, the United States carried out simultaneous strikes against terrorist facilities and infrastructure in Afghanistan. Our forces targeted one of the most active terrorist bases in the world. It contained key elements of the bin Ladin network's infrastructure and has served as a training camp for literally thousands of terrorists from around the globe. We have reason to believe that a gathering of key terrorist leaders was to take place there today, thus underscoring the urgency of our actions. Our forces also attacked a factory in Sudan associated with the bin Ladin network. The factory was involved in the production of materials for chemical weapons.

The United States does not take this action lightly. Afghanistan and Sudan have been warned for years to stop harboring and supporting these terrorist groups. But countries that persistently host terrorists have no right to be safe havens. . . .

My fellow Americans, our battle against terrorism did not begin with the bombing of our embassies in Africa, nor will it end with today's strike. It will require strength, courage and endurance. We will not yield to this threat. We will meet it no matter how long it may take. This will be a long, ongoing struggle between freedom and fanaticism, between the rule of law and terrorism. We must be prepared to do all that we can for as long as we must. America is and will remain a target of terrorists precisely because we are leaders; because we act to advance peace, democracy and basic human values; because we're the most open society on earth; and because, as we have shown yet again, we take an uncompromising stand against terrorism.

But of this I am also sure; the risks from inaction to America and the world would be far greater than action, for that would embolden our enemies, leaving their ability and their willingness to strike us intact. In this case, we knew before our attack that these groups already had planned further actions against us and others.

I want to reiterate: The United States wants peace, not conflict. We want to lift lives around the world, not take them. We have worked for peace in Bosnia, in Northern Ireland, in Haiti, in the Middle East and elsewhere, but in this day, no campaign for peace can succeed without a determination to fight terrorism.

Let our actions today send this message loud and clear: There are no expendable American targets. There will be no sanctuary for terrorists. We will defend our people, our interests and our values. We will help people of all faiths in all parts of the world who want to live free of fear and violence. We will persist and we will prevail.

Thank you, God bless you, and may God bless our country.

U.S. Department of State, "President Clinton's Oval Office Remarks on Anti-terrorist Attacks," August 20, 1998. http://usinfo.state.gov.

DOCUMENT 9: BIN LADEN DISCUSSES HIS CONTINUING WAR AGAINST AMERICA

After President Clinton's failed 1998 missile strikes at Sudan and Afghanistan, Osama bin Laden was interviewed by journalist Rahimullah Yusufzai for Time. *In the following excerpts from this interview, Bin Laden hints that he may already possess chemical and nuclear weapons, and also insists that his use of violence against the West is justified.*

Q: What can the U.S. expect from you now?

bin Laden: Any thief or criminal or robber who enters another country in order to steal should expect to be exposed to murder at any time. For the American forces to expect anything from me, personally, reflects a very narrow perception. Muslims are angry. The Americans should expect reactions from the Muslim world that are proportionate to the injustice they inflict.

Q: The U.S. says you are trying to acquire chemical and nuclear weapons. How would you use these?

bin Laden: Acquiring weapons for the defense of Muslims is a religious duty. If I have indeed acquired these weapons, then I thank God for enabling me to do so. And if I seek to acquire these weapons, I am carrying out a duty. It would be a sin for Muslims not to try to possess the weapons that would prevent the infidels from inflicting harm on Muslims.

Q: Can you describe the U.S. air strikes on your camps?

bin Laden: The American bombardment had only shown that the world is governed by the law of the jungle. That brutal, treacherous attack killed a number of civilian Muslims. As for material damage, it was minimal. By the grace of God, the missiles were ineffective. The raid proved that the American army is going downhill in its morale. Its members are too cowardly and too fearful to meet the young people of Islam face to face.

Q: The U.S. is trying to stop the flow of funds to your organization. Has it been able to do so?

bin Laden: The U.S. knows that I have attacked it, by the grace of God, for more than ten years now. The U.S. alleges that I am fully responsible for the killing of its soldiers in Somalia. God knows that we have been pleased at the killing of American soldiers. This was achieved by the grace of God and the efforts of the mujahedin from among the Somali brothers and other Arab mujahedin who had been in Afghanistan before that. America has been trying ever since to tighten its economic blockade against us and to arrest me. It has failed. This blockade does not hurt us much. We expect to be rewarded by God.

Q: What will you do if the Taliban asks you to leave Afghanistan?

bin Laden: That is not something we foresee. We do not expect to be driven out of this land. We pray to God to make our migration a migration in His cause.

Q: Do you expect any more attacks if you stay in Afghanistan?

bin Laden: Any foreign attack on Afghanistan would not target an individual. It would not target Osama bin Laden personally. The fact is that Afghanistan, having raised the banner of Islam, has become a target for the crusader-Jewish alliance. We expect Afghanistan to be bombarded, even though the non-believers will say that they do so because of the presence of Osama. That is why we, together with our brothers, live on these mountains far away from Muslims in villages and towns, in order to spare them any harm. . . .

Q: But there are many Muslims who do not agree with your kind of violence.

bin Laden: We should fully understand our religion. Fighting is a part of our religion and our Shari'a. Those who love God and his Prophet and this religion cannot deny that. Whoever denies even a minor tenet of our religion commits the gravest sin in Islam. Those who sympathize with the infidels—such as the PLO [Palestine Liberation Organization] in Palestine, or the so-called Palestinian Authority—have been trying for tens of years to get back some of their rights. They laid down arms and abandoned what is called "violence" and tried peaceful bargaining. What did the Jews give them? They did not give them even 1% of their rights.

Q: America, the world's only superpower, has called you Public

Enemy Number One. Are you worried?

bin Laden: Hostility toward America is a religious duty, and we hope to be rewarded for it by God. To call us Enemy Number One or Two does not hurt us. Osama bin Laden is confident that the Islamic nation will carry out its duty. I am confident that Muslims will be able to end the legend of the so-called superpower that is America.

Rahimullah Yusufzai, "Exclusive Interview: 'Conversation With Terror,'" January 11, 1999. www.time.com.

DOCUMENT 10: COUNTERTERRORISM CHIEF RICHARD CLARKE WARNS AGAINST THE AL QAEDA THREAT

On January 25, 2001, five days after President George W. Bush took office, counterterrorism chief Richard Clarke issued the following classified memo to national security adviser Condoleezza Rice. A holdover from President Bill Clinton's administration, Clarke attempted to draw the new administration's attention to al Qaeda (here, al Qida). The meeting Clarke urgently recommended in the memo did not take place until September 4, 2001. This memo was declassified on April 7, 2004. The symbols [***] indicate where words or passages have been blacked out for security reasons.

Just some Terrorist Group?

As we noted in our briefings for you, *al Qida* is not some narrow, little terrorist issue that needs to be included in broader regional policy. Rather, several of our regional policies need to address centrally the transnational challenge to the US and our interests posed by the *al Qida* network. By proceeding with separate policy reviews on Central Asia, the GCC [Gulf Cooperation Council], North Africa, etc. we would deal inadequately with the need for a comprehensive multi-regional policy on *al Qida.*

al Qida is the active, organized, major force that is using a distorted version of Islam as its vehicle to achieve two goals:

• to drive the US out of the Muslim world, forcing the withdrawal of our military and economic presence in countries from Morocco to Indonesia;

• to replace moderate, modern, Western regimes in Muslim countries with theocracies modeled along the lines of the Taliban [the former strict Muslim government of Afghanistan].

al Qida affects centrally our policies on Pakistan, Afghanistan, Central Asia, North Africa and the GCC. Leaders in Jordan and Saudi Arabia see *al Qida* as a direct threat to them. The strength of the network of organizations limits the scope of support friendly Arab regimes can give to a range of US policies, including Iraq policy and the [Arab-Israeli] Peace Process. We would make a major error if we underestimated the challenge *al Qida* poses, or overestimated the stability of the moderate, friendly regimes *al Qida* threatens.

Pending Time Sensitive Decisions

At the close of the Clinton Administration, two decisions about *al Qida* were deferred to the Bush Administration.

• *First, should we provide the Afghan Northern Alliance enough assistance to maintain it as a viable opposition force to the Taliban/ al Qida?* If we do not, I believe that the Northern Alliance may be effectively taken out of action this Spring when fighting resumes after the winter thaw. The *al Qida* 55th brigade, which has been a key fighting force for the Taliban, would then be freed to send its personnel elsewhere, where they would likely threaten US interests. For any assistance to get there in time to affect the Spring fighting, a decision is needed now.

• *Second, Should we increase assistance to Uzbekistan to allow them to deal with the al Qida/IMU threat?* [***]

Three other issues awaiting addressal now are:

• First, what the new Administration says to the Taliban and Pakistan about the importance we attach to ending the *al Qida* sanctuary in Afghanistan. We are separately proposing early, strong messages to both.

• Second, do we propose significant program growth in the FY02 [Fiscal Year 2002] budget for anti-*al Qida* operations by CIA and counter-terrorism training and assistance by [the Department of] State and CIA?

• Third, when and how does the Administration choose to respond to the attack on the USS *Cole* [in Yemen on October 12, 2000]. That decision is obviously complex. We can make some decisions, such as those above, now without yet coming to grips with the harder decision about the *Cole*. On the *Cole*, we should take advantage of the policy that we "will respond at a time, place, and manner of our own choosing" and not be forced into knee jerk responses.

Attached is the year-end 2000 strategy on *al Qida* developed by the last Administration to give to you. Also attached is the 1998 strategy. Neither was a "covert action only" approach. Both incorporated diplomatic, economic, military, public diplomacy and intelligence tools. Using the 2000 paper as background, we could prepare a decision paper/guide for a PC [program coordination] review.

I recommend that you have a Principals discussion of *al Qida* soon and address the following issues:

1. *Threat Magnitude:* Do the Principals agree that the *al Qida* network poses a first order threat to US interests in a number of regions, or is this analysis a "chicken little" over-reaching and can we proceed without major new initiatives and by handling this issue in a more routine manner?

2. *Strategy:* If it is a first order issue, how should the existing strategy be modified or strengthened?

Two elements of the existing strategy that have not been made to work effectively are a) going after *al Qida*'s money and b) public information to counter *al Qida* propaganda.

3. *FY02 Budget:* Should we continue the funding increases into FY02 for State and CIA programs designed to implement the *al Qida* strategy?

4. *Immediate [***] Decisions:* Should we initiate [***] funding to the Northern Alliance and to the Uzbeks?

Please let us know if you would like such a decision/discussion paper or any modifications to the background paper.

The National Security Archive, "Bush Administration's First Memo on al-Qaeda Declassified," February 10, 2005. www.gwu.edu.

DOCUMENT 11: THE TALIBAN REFUSES TO TURN OVER BIN LADEN

After Osama bin Laden went to Afghanistan in 1996, the Taliban seized control of the country and offered the al Qaeda leader unlimited protection—much to the frustration of the United States government, which made more than thirty efforts to have him expelled. The following is the introduction to a secret State Department summary circulated in July 2001. The document was declassified in 2003.

Since the Taliban captured Kabul in 1996, the United States has consistently discussed with them peace, humanitarian assistance, drugs and human rights. However, we have made clear that Usama bin Laden (UBL) and terrorism is the preeminent issue between the U.S. and the Taliban.

• These concerns over bin Ladin preceded the 1998 bombings.

• For instance, Secretary [of State Warren] Christopher wrote to the Taliban Foreign Minister in 1996 that "we wish to work with you to expel all terrorists and those who support terrorism. . ."

In our talks we have stressed that UBL has murdered Americans and continues to plan attacks against Americans and others and that we cannot ignore this threat.

• Have also emphasized that the international community shares this concern. In 1999 and in 2000, the UN Security Council passed resolutions demanding that UBL be expelled to a country where he can be brought to justice.

• Have told the Taliban that the terrorist problem is not confined to bin Laden and that the Taliban must take steps to shut down all terrorist activities.

• Have told them that the resolution of the bin Laden issue and steps to close the terrorist apparatus would enable us to discuss other issues in an improved atmosphere.

• Conversely, have stressed that if this terrorism issue is not addressed, there can be no improvement in relations.

These talks have been fruitless. The Taliban usually said that they want a solution but cannot comply with UNSCRs [UN Security Council Resolutions]. Often the Taliban asked the U.S. to suggest a solution.

• In October 1999, the Taliban suggested several "solutions" in-cluding a UBL trial by a panel of Islamic scholars or monitoring of UBL [in] Afghanistan by OIC [Organization of Islamic Conferences] or UN.

• Taliban consistently maintained that UBL's activities are re-stricted, despite all evidence to the contrary.

Often our discussions have been followed by Taliban declara-tions that no evidence exists against UBL and that he will not be expelled as demanded by the UN resolutions.

The National Security Archive, "U.S. Engagement with the Taliban on Usama Bin Laden," ca. July 16, 2001. www.gwu.edu.

DOCUMENT 12: JOURNALIST PETER L. BERGEN FEARS ATTACKS AGAINST AMERICA

Three weeks before the attacks of September 11, 2001, CNN journal-ist Peter L. Bergen viewed an al Qaeda propaganda videotape which seemed virtually to promise such attacks. He wrote a letter to New York Times *reporter John Burns summing up his concerns. After viewing the tape, Burns wrote a story about it, which* The New York Times *refused to print. As Bergen later wrote, "The last, best warning to America of what might be ahead failed to see the light of day." An abridged version of Bergen's letter to Burns is reprinted here.*

August 17, 2001

John,

I think there is a major story to be told wrapping around the new bin Laden videotape and the various threats against U.S. facil-ities in past months which can paint both a compelling picture of the bin Laden organization today, and responsibly suggest that an al-Qaeda attack is in the works. . . . As you know there were very strong indications of attacks on U.S. targets in Yemen in June. Also in June two men were picked up in New Delhi, who said they were planning to blow up the busy visa section of the U.S. embassy. . . . On July 18, the State Department issued a statement that the USG [U.S. government] has "strong indications that individuals may be planning imminent terrorist actions against U.S. interests in the Arabian Peninsula."

Clearly, al-Qaeda was and is planning something.

Now comes the two-hour bin Laden recruitment-propaganda tape, brief snippets of which were shown on CNN and Reuters ran a story about it when it surfaced in Kuwait in late June. But no one has looked at the entire tape, or if they have, they did not bother to sit down and translate the whole thing. . . .

Also no one has thought to put the videotape in the context of al-Qaeda's modus operandi which is to subtly indicate a plot is in the works before it takes place. We saw this in May 1998 when bin Laden held a press conference in Afghanistan where he talked of "good news in coming weeks" and a few days later told ABC News that he predicted a "black day for America." Nine weeks later the embassies in Africa [Tanzania and Kenya] were bombed. . . .

A few months before the [USS] *Cole* bombing [in Yemen, October 12, 2000] as you know, a tape appeared which is notable for two things: bin Laden is wearing the *jambiya* Yemeni dagger [a dagger with a curved blade] which he had never previously worn in any of the dozens of photos that exist of him, and his deputy Ayman al-Zawahiri specifically called for attacks on American forces in Yemen. This tape is of more than passing interest to U.S. investigators, and again shows how al-Qaeda subtly signals its next move.

Now the videotape I have in hand is circulating around the Middle East, which has all sorts of juicy stuff on it detailed below, not least of which is that on the tape bin Laden makes a set of statements taking credit for a number of anti-American actions, his most explicit and wide-ranging to date. . . .

On the tape, bin Laden and his advisers make impassioned speeches about Muslims being attacked in Chechnya, Kashmir, Iraq, Israel, Lebanon, Indonesia, and Egypt; speeches which are laid over graphic footage of Muslims being killed, beaten, and imprisoned. The videotape devotes ten to fifteen minutes to images of Palestinians under attack by Israeli soldiers. . . .

For bin Laden, however, the greatest insult to Muslims is the continued presence of Americans in the holy land of Arabia. Bin Laden says: "These Americans brought women and Jewish women who can go anywhere in our holy land" adding "the Arab rulers worship the God of the White House." These statements are made over images of Saudi royal family members meeting American leaders such as Colin Powell.

Bin Laden says that Muslims must seek revenge for these insults: "If you don't fight you will be punished by God." The Saudi exile says the solution to these problems is that Muslims should travel to Afghanistan, and receive training about how to do jihad. The tape then shows hundreds of bin Laden's masked followers training at his al-Farouq camp in eastern Afghanistan, holding up black flags and chanting in Arabic "fight evil." Bin Laden's fighters shoot off anti-aircraft guns and RPGs [rocket-propelled grenades], hold up their Korans and their Kalashnikovs [AK-47s], run across obstacle courses, dive into pools of water, blow up buildings and shoot at images of President Clinton. Bin Laden himself looses off some rounds from an automatic rifle. Chillingly, the tape also shows dozens of young boys, most of whom appear to be around ten, dressed in military camouflage uniforms, chanting for jihad. . . .

Towards the end of the tape, bin Laden implies more action against the United States: "The victory of Islam is coming. And the victory of Yemen will continue. . . ." The entire video is now available in a DVD format and is also circulating in clandestine chat rooms on the Internet, according to those familiar with bin Laden's organization . . . [who also say] "these threats on the videotape are genuine, that bin Laden's followers are making real preparations against more than one American target."

Peter L. Bergen, *Holy War, Inc.: Inside the Secret World of Osama bin Laden.* New York: Touchstone, 2002; pp. 26–28.

DOCUMENT 13: PRESIDENT BUSH SEEKS JUSTICE

On September 17, 2001, less than a week after the 9/11 attacks, President George W. Bush talked to members of the Pentagon press corps about preparations for a war against terrorism. In the following excerpt from his question-and-answer session with reporters, Bush speculated about the unusual nature of the impending conflict.

Q: Mr. President, is it the case, based on what you've said now, that war is inevitable, and can you tell the American people what that war is going to look like?

Bush: I believe, I know that an act of war was declared against America. But this will be a different type of war than we're used to. This is—in the past there have been beaches to storm and islands to conquer. We've been able to watch on our television screens sophisticated weaponry find a building; and we've seen dramatic reports from the front where Pulitzer Prize-to-be winning reporters stood up and declared, the United States is attacked, and all that.

There may be some of that, who knows. But I know that this is a different type of enemy than we're used to. It's an enemy that likes to hide and burrow in, and their network is extensive. There are no rules. It's barbaric behavior. They slit throats of women on airplanes in order to achieve an objective that is beyond comprehension. And they like to hit, and then they like to hide out.

But we're going to smoke them out. And we're adjusting our thinking to the new type of enemy. These are terrorists who have no borders. And, by the way, it's important for the world to understand that we know in America that more than just Americans suffered loss of life in the World Trade Center. People from all kinds of nationalities lost—that's why the world is rallying to our call to defeat terrorism.

Many world leaders understand that that could have easily— that the attack could have as easily happened on their land. And they also understand that this enemy knows no border. But they know what I know, that when we start putting the heat on those who house them, they will get them running. And once we get them running we have got a good chance of getting them. And that's exactly what our intent is.

The focus right now is on Osama bin Laden, no question about it. He's the prime suspect, and his organization. But there are other terrorists in the world. There are people who hate freedom. This is a fight for freedom. This is a fight to say to the freedom-loving people of the world: we will not allow ourselves to be terrorized by somebody who thinks they can hit and hide in some cave somewhere.

It's going to require a new thought process. And I'm proud to report our military, led by the Secretary of Defense [Donald Rumsfeld], understands that; understands it's a new type of war, it's going to take a long time to win this war. The American people are going to have to be more patient than ever with the efforts of—our combined efforts, not just ourselves, but the efforts of our allies, to get them running and find them and to hunt them down.

But as the Vice President [Richard B. Cheney] said, you know, Osama bin Laden is just one person. He is representative of networks of people who absolutely have made their cause to defeat the freedoms that we take—that we understand. And we will not allow them to do so.

Q: Do you want bin Laden dead?

Bush: I want justice. There's an old poster out west, as I recall, that said, "Wanted: Dead or Alive."

Q: Do you see this being long-term? You were saying it's long-term, do you see an end, at all?

Bush: I think that this is a long-term battle, war. There will be battles. But this is long-term. After all, our mission is not just Osama bin Laden, the al Qaeda organization. Our mission is to battle terrorism and to join with freedom loving people.

We are putting together a coalition that is a coalition dedicated to declaring to the world we will do what it takes to find the terrorists, to rout them out and to hold them accountable. And the United States is proud to lead the coalition.

Q: Are you saying you want him dead or alive, sir? Can I interpret—

Bush: I just remember, all I'm doing is remembering when I was a kid I remember that they used to put out there in the old west, a wanted poster. It said: "Wanted, Dead or Alive." All I want and America wants him brought to justice. That's what we want.

George W. Bush, "Guard and Reserves 'Define Spirit of America,'" September 17, 2001. www.whitehouse.gov.

DOCUMENT 14: THE TALIBAN'S MULLAH OMAR PROTECTS BIN LADEN EVEN AFTER 9/11

Even after the attacks of 9/11, the Taliban's leader Mullah Omar refused to expel Osama bin Laden from Afghanistan. He explained his reasons in the following interview with the publicly funded radio channel Voice of America.

Q: Why don't you expel Osama bin Laden?

Omar: This is not an issue of Osama bin Laden. It is an issue of Islam. Islam's prestige is at stake. So is Afghanistan's tradition.

Q: Do you know that the US has announced a war on terrorism?

Omar: I am considering two promises. One is the promise of

God, the other is that of Bush. The promise of God is that my land is vast. If you start a journey on God's path, you can reside anywhere on this earth and will be protected. . . . The promise of Bush is that there is no place on earth where you can hide that I cannot find you. We will see which one of these two promises is fulfilled.

Q: But aren't you afraid for the people, yourself, the Taliban, your country?

Omar: Almighty God . . . is helping the believers and the Muslims. God says he will never be satisfied with the infidels. In terms of worldly affairs, America is very strong. Even if it were twice as strong or twice that, it could not be strong enough to defeat us. We are confident that no one can harm us if God is with us.

Q: You are telling me you are not concerned, but Afghans all over the world are concerned.

Omar: We are also concerned. Great issues lie ahead. But we depend on God's mercy. Consider our point of view: if we give Osama away today, Muslims who are now pleading to give him up would then be reviling us for giving him up. . . . Everyone is afraid of America and wants to please it. But Americans will not be able to prevent such acts like the one that has just occurred because America has taken Islam hostage. If you look at Islamic countries, the people are in despair. They are complaining that Islam is gone. But people remain firm in their Islamic beliefs. In their pain and frustration, some of them commit suicide acts. They feel they have nothing to lose.

Q: What do you mean by saying America has taken the Islamic world hostage?

Omar: America controls the governments of the Islamic countries. The people ask to follow Islam, but the governments do not listen because they are in the grip of the United States. If someone follows the path of Islam, the government arrests him, tortures him or kills him. This is the doing of America. If it stops supporting those governments and lets the people deal with them, then such things won't happen. America has created the evil that is attacking it. The evil will not disappear even if I die and Osama dies and others die. The US should step back and review its policy. It should stop trying to impose its empire on the rest of the world, especially on Islamic countries.

Q: So you won't give Osama bin Laden up?

Omar: No. We cannot do that. If we did, it means we are not Muslims . . . that Islam is finished. If we were afraid of attack, we could have surrendered him the last time we were threatened and attacked. So America can hit us again, and this time we don't even have a friend.

Q: If you fight America with all your might—can the Taliban do that? Won't America beat you and won't your people suffer even more?

Omar: I'm very confident that it won't turn out this way. Please note this: there is nothing more we can do except depend on

almighty God. If a person does, then he is assured that the Almighty
will help him, have mercy on him and he will succeed.

Guardian Unlimited (UK), "Mullah Omar: In His Own Words," September 26, 2001.
www.guardian.co.uk.

DOCUMENT 15: PRESIDENT BUSH SAYS THAT THE U.S. MISSION IS NOT MERELY ABOUT HUNTING DOWN BIN LADEN

*By early 2002, U.S.-led military forces had driven the Taliban from
power in Afghanistan. Many al Qaeda members had been killed or
captured, and Osama bin Laden himself was thought to be either
dead or in hiding. During a March 13 White House press conference,
excerpted below, President George W. Bush stated that the al Qaeda
threat had been reduced and that Osama bin Laden's role had been
"marginalized" in the war on terror.*

Q: Mr. President, in your speeches now you rarely talk [of] or mention Osama bin Laden. Why is that? Also, can you tell the American
people if you have any more information, if you know if he is dead
or alive? Final part—deep in your heart, don't you truly believe that
until you find out if he is dead or alive, you won't really eliminate
the threat of—

Bush: Deep in my heart I know the man is on the run, if he's
alive at all. Who knows if he's hiding in some cave or not; we
haven't heard from him in a long time. And the idea of focusing on
one person is—really indicates to me people don't understand the
scope of the mission.

Terror is bigger than one person. And he's just—he's a person
who's now been marginalized. His network, his host government
has been destroyed. He's the ultimate parasite who found weakness, exploited it, and met his match. He is—as I mentioned in my
speech, I do mention the fact that this is a fellow who is willing to
commit youngsters to their death and he, himself, tries to hide—if,
in fact, he's hiding at all.

So I don't know where he is. You know, I just don't spend that
much time on him . . . to be honest with you. I'm more worried
about making sure that our soldiers are well-supplied; that the
strategy is clear; that the coalition is strong; that when we find enemy bunched up like we did in Shahikot Mountains [early in
March 2002], that the military has all the support it needs to go in
and do the job, which they did.

And there will be other battles in Afghanistan. There's going to
be other struggles like Shahikot, and I'm just as confident about the
outcome of those future battles as I was about Shahikot, where our
soldiers are performing brilliantly. We're tough, we're strong, they're
well-equipped. We have a good strategy. We are showing the world
we know how to fight a guerrilla war with conventional means.

Q: But don't you believe that the threat that bin Laden posed won't truly be eliminated until he is found either dead or alive?

Bush: Well, as I say, we haven't heard much from him. And I wouldn't necessarily say he's at the center of any command structure. And, again, I don't know where he is. I—I'll repeat what I said. I truly am not that concerned about him. I know he is on the run. I was concerned about him, when he had taken over a country. I was concerned about the fact that he was basically running Afghanistan and calling the shots for the Taliban.

But once we set out the policy and started executing the plan, he became—we shoved him out more and more on the margins. He has no place to train his al Qaeda killers anymore. And if we—excuse me for a minute—and if we find a training camp, we'll take care of it. Either we will or our friends will. That's one of the things—part of the new phase that's becoming apparent to the American people is that we're working closely with other governments to deny sanctuary, or training, or a place to hide, or a place to raise money.

And we've got more work to do. See, that's the thing the American people have got to understand, that we've only been at this six months. This is going to be a long struggle. I keep saying that; I don't know whether you all believe me or not. But time will show you that it's going to take a long time to achieve this objective. And I can assure you, I am not going to blink. And I'm not going to get tired. Because I know what is at stake. And history has called us to action, and I am going to seize this moment for the good of the world, for peace in the world and for freedom.

U.S. Department of State, "Bush Says Israeli Actions Not Helpful in Peace Effort," March 13, 2002. http://usinfo.state.gov.

DOCUMENT 16: BIN LADEN URGES IRAQIS TO RESIST AN AMERICAN INVASION

On March 20, 2003, U.S.-led forces invaded Iraq to overthrow Saddam Hussein's regime. A little more than a month before the invasion, Osama bin Laden issued an audiotaped message, excerpted here. Although Bin Laden had long opposed Saddam's secular, socialist government, he now encouraged Iraqis in their impending war with America, advising them to employ the trench warfare tactics he had used during the battle of Tora Bora in December 2001. He also urged guerrilla attacks by Islamists worldwide.

O mujahideen [holy warrior] brothers in Iraq, do not be afraid of what the United States is propagating in terms of their lies about their power and their smart, laser-guided missiles.

The smart bombs will have no effect worth mentioning in the hills and in the trenches, on plains, and in forests.

They must have apparent targets. The well-camouflaged trenches and targets will not be reached by either the smart or the stupid missiles.

There will only be haphazard strikes that dissipate the enemy ammunition and waste its money. Dig many trenches.

The [early Muslim caliph] Umar, may God be pleased with him, stated: "Take the ground as a shield because this will ensure the exhaustion of all the stored enemy missiles within months."

Their daily production is too little and can be dealt with, God willing.

We also recommend luring the enemy forces into a protracted, close, and exhausting fight, using the camouflaged defensive positions in plains, farms, mountains, and cities.

The enemy fears city and street wars most, a war in which the enemy expects grave human losses.

We stress the importance of the martyrdom operations against the enemy—operations that inflicted harm on the United States and Israel that have been unprecedented in their history, thanks to Almighty God.

We also point out that whoever supported the United States, including the hypocrites of Iraq or the rulers of Arab countries, those who approved their actions and followed them in this crusade war by fighting with them or providing bases and administrative support, or any form of support, even by words, to kill the Muslims in Iraq, should know that they are apostates and outside the community of Muslims.

It is permissible to spill their blood and take their property.

God says: "O ye who believe! Take not the Jews and the Christians for your friends and protectors: they are but friends and protectors to each other."

And he amongst you that turns to them [for friendship] is of them.

Verily, Allah guideth not a people unjust.

We also stress to honest Muslims that they should move, incite, and mobilize the [Islamic] nation, amid such grave events and hot atmosphere so as to liberate themselves from those unjust and renegade ruling regimes, which are enslaved by the United States.

They should also do so to establish the rule of God on earth.

The most qualified regions for liberation are Jordan, Morocco, Nigeria, Pakistan, the land of the two holy mosques [Saudi Arabia], and Yemen.

Needless to say, this crusade war is primarily targeted against the people of Islam.

Regardless of the removal or the survival of the socialist party or Saddam, Muslims in general and the Iraqis in particular must brace themselves for jihad against this unjust campaign and acquire ammunition and weapons.

This is a prescribed duty. God says: "[And let them pray with thee] taking all precautions and bearing arms: the unbelievers wish if ye were negligent of your arms and your baggage, to assault you in a single rush."

Fighting in support of the non-Islamic banners is forbidden.

Muslims' doctrine and banner should be clear in fighting for the sake of God. He who fights to raise the word of God will fight for God's sake.

Under these circumstances, there will be no harm if the interests of Muslims converge with the interests of the socialists in the fight against the crusaders, despite our belief in the infidelity of socialists.

The jurisdiction of the socialists and those rulers has fallen a long time ago.

Socialists are infidels wherever they are, whether they are in Baghdad or Aden.

BBC News, Test of bin Laden audio message broadcast on al-Jazeera, February 12, 2003. http://news.bbc.co.uk.

DOCUMENT 17: BIN LADEN'S PEACE OFFER TO EUROPE

In 2003, Osama bin Laden threatened to conduct terrorist strikes against nations serving in the U.S.-led coalition in Iraq—Spain and Great Britain among them. On March 11, 2004, a series of commuter train explosions rocked Madrid, Spain, killing nearly two hundred people and wounding more than eighteen hundred. Carried out by Islamic extremists with possible al Qaeda connections, the bombings were carefully scheduled to influence Spain's upcoming election. On March 14, Spanish voters ousted the government that had supported the United States in Iraq. In the following announcement, Osama bin Laden praises the success of the attacks, while offering peace to any European nation that refuses to cooperate with America.

This is a message to our neighbors north of the Mediterranean, with a proposal for a peace treaty, in response to the positive reactions which emerged there.

What happened in September 11 and March 11 is your own merchandise coming back to you. We hereby advise you . . . that your definition of us and of our actions as terrorism is nothing but a definition of yourselves by yourselves, since our reaction is of the same kind as your act. Our actions are a reaction to yours, which are destruction and killing of our people as is happening in Afghanistan, Iraq, and Palestine.

It suffices to see the event that shocked the world—the killing of the wheelchair-bound old man *Ahmad Yassin* [leader of the Palestinian movement Hamas, killed by Israelis in 2004]—Allah's mercy upon him—and we pledge to Allah to avenge [his murder] on America, Allah willing.

By what measure of kindness are your killed considered innocents while ours are considered worthless? By what school [of thought] is your blood considered blood while our blood is water?

Therefore, it is [only] just to respond in kind, and the one who started it is more to blame. . . .

When you look at what happened and is happening, the killing in our countries and in yours, an important fact emerges, and that is that the oppression is forced on both us and you by your politicians who send your sons, against your will, to our country to kill and to be killed.

Therefore, both sides have an interest in thwarting those who shed the blood of the peoples for their own narrow interests, out of vassalage to the White House gang. . . .

This war makes millions of dollars for big corporations, either weapons manufacturers or those working in the reconstruction [of Iraq], such as [multinational corporation] *Halliburton* and its sister companies. . . .

It is crystal clear who benefits from igniting the fire of this war and this bloodshed: They are the merchants of war, the bloodsuckers who run the policy of the world from behind the scenes.

President [George W.] Bush and his ilk, the media giants, and the U.N. . . . all are a fatal danger to the world, and the Zionist lobby is their most dangerous member. Allah willing, we will persist in fighting them. . . .

Therefore, in order to thwart opportunities for the merchants of war, and in response to the positive developments that were expressed in recent events and in the public opinion polls, which determined that most European peoples want peace, I urge . . . the establishment of a permanent commission to nurture awareness among Europeans regarding the justness of our causes, particularly the cause of Palestine, and that use be made of the vast media resources to this end.

I hereby offer them a peace treaty, the essence of which is our commitment to halt actions against any country that commits itself to refraining from attacking Muslims or intervening in their affairs, including the American conspiracy against the larger Islamic world.

This peace treaty can be renewed at the end of the term of a government and the rise of another, with the agreement of both sides.

The peace treaty will be in force upon the exit of the last soldier of any given [European] country from our land.

The door of peace will remain open for three months from the broadcast of this statement. Whoever rejects the peace and wants war should know that we are the men [of war], and whoever wants a peace treaty and signs it, we hereby allow this peace treaty with him.

Stop shedding our blood in order to protect your own blood. The solution to this easy-difficult equation is in your own hands. You should know that the longer you delay, the worse the situation will become, and when that happens, do not blame us, blame yourselves. . . .

As for those who lie to people and say that we hate freedom and kill for the sake of killing—reality proves that we are the speakers of truth and they lie, because the killing of the Russians took place only after their invasion of Afghanistan and Chechnya; the killing of the Europeans took place only after the invasion of Iraq and Afghanistan; the killing of the Americans in the Battle of New York took place only after their support for the Jews in Palestine and their invasion of the Arabian Peninsula; their killing in Somalia happened only after *Operation Restore Hope* [in the early 1990s]. We restored [i.e., repelled] them without hope, by the grace of Allah.

Osama bin Laden, speech offering peace to European countries that withdraw from Arab lands. The Middle East Media Research Institute, Special Dispatch Series—No. 695, April 15, 2004. www.memri.org.

DOCUMENT 18: A FATWA AGAINST OSAMA BIN LADEN

To mark the first anniversary of the Madrid commuter train bombings of March 11, 2004, the Islamic Commission of Spain issued a remarkable document—the first legitimate fatwa (decree) against Osama bin Laden and al Qaeda. The 2005 fatwa was signed by the commission's secretary general, Mansur Escudero Bedate, who said that it was supported by Islamic religious authorities in Morocco, Algeria, and Libya. The following excerpt condemns terrorist acts. Numbered references are to passages in the Koran and various hadiths (collections of sayings and deeds of Mohammed).

The [proper] concept of war established in the Koran has an exclusively defensive tone:

> "and you fight for the cause of God against those who fight you, but you do not commit aggressions, since certainly, God does not love the aggressors" (2:190).

As [the author and Jewish convert to Islam] Muhammad Asad in his *tafsir* (interpretation of the Koran) says: "Most commentators agree that the expression *taatadu* means, in this context, "you do not commit aggression". The defensive character of combat "for the cause of God"—that is to say, because of the ethical principles ordered by God, is evident by the reference to "those who fight you" . . . and it is clarified furthermore in the *aleya* [law] 22:39: "It is allowed (to fight) those who have injured them unjustly"; that is, according to all our traditions, our first (and therefore fundamental) Koranic reference to the question of yihad" [i.e., jihad].

Within the context of defensive warfare, The Prophet imposed strict limits destined to safeguard lives and properties. Thus, the Prophet Muhammad prohibited to kill, in the case of warlike conflict, women, children and civilians (Sahih Muslim:1744, and Sahih Al-Bujari: 3015).

He also said whosoever killed anyone who had signed a treaty or agreement with Muslims, would not smell the fragrance of Paradise (Sahih Al-Bujari:3166, and Ibn Mayah:2686).

In light of these and other Islamic texts, the terrorist acts of Osama ben Laden and his organization Al Qaida—who look to fill with fear the hearts of defenseless people; who engage in the destruction of buildings or properties thus involving the death of civilians, like women, children, and other beings—are strictly prohibited and are the object of a full condemnation from Islam.

Therefore, the perpetration of terrorist acts under the pretext "of defending the oppressed nations of the world or the rights of Muslims" does not have any justification in Islam.

There is no doubt Muslims have the legitimate right to react against any aggression or any situation of oppression. Nevertheless, such reaction should not give rise to blind or irrational hatred:

> "you do not let your hatred towards those who prevent you access to the House of Inviolable Adoration (that is to say, to the fulfillment of your religious obligations) take you to transgression (the limits); but on the contrary, [it should encourage you to] collaborate in fomenting virtue and acknowledgment of God and not to collaborate in fomenting evil and enmity." (5:2)

Likewise, the Koran indicates, in reference to those who hypocritically claim to follow the Bible, that whenever anyone lights the fire of war, God extinguishes it (5:64). God also condemns those nations that violate international treaties and initiate wars (8:56) and requests that everything is done to defeat them (8:60), but if they are inclined to peace, then Muslims will have to follow suit as well. (8:61).

Given all of this, it is necessary to point out that terrorism and extremism contradict human nature and the lessons of Islam.

Muslims must know that terrorism is a threat against Islam and that it's damaging to our religion and to Muslims. A correct Islamic formation in *madrasas* [religious schools] and Islamic universities will allow everybody to understand that Islam is a religion of peace and that it repudiates all acts of terrorism and indiscriminate death.

The presence of signs like arrogance, fanaticism, extremism or religious intolerance in an individual or group, lets us know they have broken with Islam and the traditions of the Prophet Muhammad.

The perpetration of terrorist acts supposes a rupture of such magnitude with Islamic teaching that it allows to affirm that the individuals or groups who have perpetrated them have stopped being Muslim and have put themselves outside the sphere of Islam. Such groups distort and manipulate basic Islamic concepts, like the one of *yihad*, by imposing upon them their particular interpretation and criteria.

In fact, groups that use names and languages relative to Islam, discredit with their actions the image of Islam and serve the interests of their enemies. Their actions incite islamophobia in countries in which Muslims are a minority, and destroy the relationships of cooperation and neighborliness between Muslims and non-Muslims. Their actions provide a false image of Islam, which is precisely what the enemies of Islam strive to offer to the world.

These extremist groups bring indiscriminate death, even to other Muslims. We must remember here that The Prophet showed that Muslims who kill other Muslims turn *kafir* (unbelieving).

In this same sense, if a Muslim or a group of them commit a terrorist act, this individual or group would be breaking the laws of Islam and leaving the guide of God and the way of the *Din* [obedience or submission].

> "God does not grant his guidance to people who deliberately do evil."
> (9:109).

Islamic Commission of Spain, fatwa declared against Osama bin Laden, trans. Liza Sabater, March 12, 2005. www.culturekitchen.com.

DOCUMENT 19: FATWA ACCUSES OSAMA BIN LADEN OF CONTRADICTING DIVINE DECREE

The following concluding excerpts from the 2005 Spanish fatwa accuse Osama bin Laden and al Qaeda of istihlal—*making up one's own laws. It also condemns Bin Laden's dream of a Caliphate (pan-Islamic state) that would include Andalusia, or southern Spain. The document closes by declaring Bin Laden and his followers to be apostates of Islam.*

Based on what has been exposed, it comes to dictate:

That according to the Sharia [Islamic law], all who declare *halal* or allowed what God has declared *haram* or prohibited, like the killing of innocent people in terrorist attacks, have become *Kafir Murtadd Mustahlil*, that's to say an apostate, by trying to make a crime such as the murder of innocents, *halal* (istihlal); a crime forbidden by the Sacred Koran and the Sunna [sayings and deeds] of the Prophet Muhammad, God bless him and save him.

As long as Osama ben Laden and his organization defend the legality of terrorism and try to base it on the Sacred Koran and the Sunna, they are committing the crime of *istihlal* and they have become ipso facto apostates (*kafir murtadd*), who should not be considered Muslim nor be treated as such.

To which we declare that Osama ben Laden and his organization Al Qaida, responsible for the horrible crimes against the innocents who vilely were assassinated in the terrorist attack of 11 March in Madrid, are outside the parameters of Islam; and the same goes to all who wield the Sacred Koran and The Prophet's Sunna to commit terrorist acts.

To which we declare that the alleged political reasonings by Osama ben Laden and his organization regarding the recovery of *Al Andalus* [Andalusia]; having been made public and become well-known by all, completely contradict the divine will that has been expressed clearly through history; being that God is the Lord of History and everything that happens, has happened or will happen; that he is Divine Aim and Favor and must be considered as such in any event by Muslims, for whom God is Giver of Goods; and that not even the best of conspirators are creatures with the capacity to judge or question what the Divine Will has decreed.

The tragedy of *Al Andalus*, the genocide of Muslims and their expulsion from Spain, the natural mother country of all of them, is to be judged by God alone; and to the servant, to accept the Divine Decree and be thankful. . . .

Based on this fatwa, we have requested the national government and Spanish mass media to stop using the words *Islam* or *Islamic* to describe these malefactors, given they are not Muslim nor have any relationship with our Umma or Islamic Community; instead needing to call them Al Qaida terrorists, but without using Islamic as an adjective, since as it has been declared above, they are not legally so.

Likewise, we ask those in charge of mass media to acknowledge what has been stated here and to proceed from now on under the criteria exposed above; particularly, by not tying Islam nor Muslims with any terrorist acts; especially if the acts appear dressed with any Islamic language or pretension.

Islamic Commission of Spain, fatwa declared against Osama bin Laden, trans. Liza Sabater, March 12, 2005. www.culturekitchen.com.

DISCUSSION QUESTIONS

CHAPTER 1

1. Jason Burke describes Osama bin Laden's childhood, emphasizing his relationships with family members, his affluence and privilege, and also his father's stern religious and work ethic. How do you think these aspects of his younger days contributed to Bin Laden's development into an Islamic extremist?

2. Yossef Bodanksy asserts that, as a youth, Bin Laden was "a drinker and womanizer, which often got him into bar brawls." Peter L. Bergen and some other experts question this widely accepted view, believing instead that Bin Laden was upright in his behavior and deeply religious even as a youngster. Which viewpoint do you find more persuasive? From what you know of Bin Laden's activities as an adult, do you find it easier to believe Bodansky or Bergen? Explain.

3. Yossef Bodanksy discusses events in the Islamic world that took place while Bin Laden was growing up, including the assassination of Saudi Arabia's King Faisal, Egyptian president Anwar Sadat's peace agreement with Israel, the seizure by militants of the Grand Mosque in Mecca, and the forming of an Islamic republic in Iran. How do you think these events shaped the thinking of Bin Laden and other Islamic extremists?

4. Peter L. Bergen discusses Bin Laden's activities during the Soviet-Afghan War of 1979–1989. Based on information in Bergen's article, how much impact did Bin Laden and his Arab Afghans have on the outcome of that war? Explain how the war shaped Bin Laden's future.

CHAPTER 2

1. Based on Benjamin Orbach's article, how is al Qaeda different from other terrorist organizations? In what ways do these differences strengthen al Qaeda, and in what ways do they weaken it? Do you think Bin Laden's power over

al Qaeda and worldwide Islamic extremism is primarily administrative or symbolic? Explain your response.

2. According to Michael Scheuer, Bin Laden believed that U.S. humanitarian relief efforts in Somalia during the early 1990s were actually efforts to seize power in the region. Why do you think Bin Laden was so convinced of ill intentions on America's part? Research U.S. involvement in Somalia to support your answer.

3. Michael Scheuer, a former CIA agent and one of the world's foremost experts on Bin Laden, has controversially claimed that Bin Laden is a "worthy enemy" who is "waging an insurgency, not a terrorist campaign." How do you see this viewpoint reflected in Scheuer's article about Bin Laden's activities in Sudan? How do you define the word *terrorist*? Should this word be applied to Bin Laden? Why or why not?

4. Summarize al Qaeda's historical account of the struggle between Islam and the West as related in "Military Studies in the Jihad Against the Tyrants." In what ways does this account strike you as accurate? In what ways does it strike you as inaccurate?

CHAPTER 3

1. Regarding the two nearly simultaneous 1998 bombings of U.S. embassies in Africa, Simon Reeve quotes a retired CIA official as saying, "Two at once is not twice as hard. Two at once is a hundred times as hard." What does the timing of the embassy bombings demonstrate about Bin Laden and al Qaeda? Why do you think Bin Laden and al Qaeda took so much trouble to stage these bombings almost simultaneously?

2. According to *The 9/11 Commission Report* of 2004, Bin Laden is said to have been disappointed that the bombing of the USS *Cole* in 2000 was not followed by U.S. attacks against al Qaeda. Why do you think he hoped for such attacks? What does this disappointment reveal about Bin Laden's goals and mindset?

3. In the days following September 11, 2001, skepticism lingered about U.S. government claims that Bin Laden was behind the attacks on America, especially since no evidence for his involvement was immediately produced. How convincing do you find the evidence presented soon after the attacks in "The Attacks of 9/11," excerpts from a British government report? What subsequent evidence has appeared that Bin Laden was involved in the attacks?

4. Imagine a conversation between Bin Laden and Esther

Sakinah Quinlan. How do you think Bin Laden would respond to Quinlan's claim that he and other extremists have distorted the Islamic concept of jihad?

CHAPTER 4

1. The U.S. government's failure to capture or kill Bin Laden, especially during the Battle of Tora Bora, has become a controversial political issue. How do you feel about America's conduct of the war on terror? Do you believe that Bin Laden is a greater or lesser threat to America now than he was before 9/11? Explain your response.

2. Certain international observers, including John Arquilla and Milt Bearden, suspect that Bin Laden's capture or death might backfire against the West, making radical Islam more dangerous to the West than ever. Considering this possibility, what do you think would constitute a true victory in the war on terror?

3. In his message to the American people of November 2004, Bin Laden threatened to bankrupt the United States. Taking into account the fact that the attacks of 9/11 cost al Qaeda several hundred thousand dollars and only nineteen lives, while costing the United States hundreds of billions of dollars and nearly three thousand lives, how seriously do you take this threat? Explain your response.

CHRONOLOGY

CA. 1930

Muhammad bin Laden, a poor construction worker, emigrates from Yemen to Jeddah, a city in what will become Saudi Arabia; for a time he works in Jeddah as a porter.

1931

Muhammad bin Laden starts a profitable construction business.

1932

The Kingdom of Saudi Arabia is founded; Muhammad bin Laden has already established close personal and business ties with the ruling al-Saud royal family; in the ensuing years, he will become a multibillionaire.

1957

Osama bin Laden is born in Riyadh, Saudi Arabia, on March 10 or July 30, the seventeenth of Muhammad bin Laden's more than fifty children and the last of his sons.

1964

Egyptian scholar Sayyid Qutb publishes his Islamist tract *Milestones* (also known as *Signposts Along the Road*), a book that will have a profound effect on Osama bin Laden and countless other radical Muslims.

1968

Muhammad bin Laden is killed in a helicopter crash.

1974

At the age of seventeen, Osama bin Laden marries his first wife; he begins his studies at King Abdul Aziz University in Jeddah, where he becomes a student of Muhammad Qutb, brother of the late author of *Milestones;* also teaching at the university is the Islamic scholar Abdullah Azzam, Bin Laden's future mentor.

1978

Israeli prime minister Menachem Begin and Egyptian president Anwar Sadat sign a peace agreement at Camp David, Maryland, with the mediation of U.S. president Jimmy Carter; Begin and Sadat win the Nobel Peace Prize for their efforts; many Arabs—including young Bin Laden—are deeply offended by the agreement, especially Sadat's acknowledgement of Israel's right to exist.

1979

Bin Laden graduates from King Abdul Aziz University.
April: The Iranian Revolution makes Ayatollah Ruhollah Khomeini the founding ruler of an Islamic republic; Bin Laden and other radical Muslims are inspired by the creation of a fundamentalist theocracy in Iran.
November: Iranian students seize the U.S. embassy in Tehran, where they hold fifty-two hostages; Islamist sentiments are also stirred when radical Muslims seize the Grand Mosque of Mecca, Saudi Arabia.
December: The Soviet Union invades Afghanistan; Bin Laden quickly goes to Afghanistan to assist the mujahideen (Islamic holy warriors) in their war against the Soviets.

1981

Bin Laden continues to travel back and forth between Saudi Arabia and the Pakistani-Afghan border, assisting the mujahideen with finances and construction projects; during the Afghan jihad (struggle) Bin Laden is reunited with Azzam; they team up to recruit and organize Afghan Arabs—Muslim fighters who have come to Afghanistan from other countries.
January 10: The U.S. embassy hostages in Tehran are released.
October 6: Egyptian president Sadat is assassinated; among those arrested after the assassination is the Egyptian radical Ayman al-Zawahiri, who will eventually become Bin Laden's right-hand man.

1987

April: Bin Laden proves himself a combat hero during the week-long Soviet assault of his military camp near Jaji, along the Pakistani-Afghan border.

1988

In Afghanistan Bin Laden begins building what the U.S. government will later dub al Qaeda (Arabic for "the base"), an organization intended to promote militant jihad worldwide.

1989

The Soviet Union withdraws its troops from Afghanistan; Bin Laden's mentor and comrade Azzam is assassinated; Bin Laden returns to Saudi Arabia, having been wounded at least twice in the Afghan conflict; he is acclaimed at home as a hero, but he also becomes an outspoken critic of the Saudi regime.

1990

August: Iraq, led by dictator Saddam Hussein, invades Kuwait; Bin Laden tries to persuade the Saudi regime to put him in charge of an Islamist army to defend Saudi Arabia from Hussein; to Bin Laden's disgust, the Saudis turn instead to the United States for help; U.S. troops arrive in Saudi Arabia on August 7.

1991

February: The U.S.-led forces drive Iraqi troops out of Kuwait; afterward, the United States maintains a strong military presence in the Arab peninsula.
April: Now regarded as a dangerous subversive by the Saudi regime, Bin Laden flees Saudi Arabia, returning to Afghanistan for a short time.

1992

Bin Laden settles in the African nation of Sudan, which is ruled by the National Islamic Front (NIF); he continues to build al Qaeda there, targeting U.S. troops involved in Operation Provide Relief (soon renamed Operation Restore Hope), a humanitarian mission for famine-stricken Somalia.
December 29: Al Qaeda carries out the bombings of two hotels in Aden, Yemen, in hopes of killing American soldiers bound for Somalia; two people are killed, neither of them Americans.

1993

February 26: A truck bomb damages the North Tower of New York's World Trade Center, killing six people; eventually, Bin Laden and al Qaeda will be linked to the attack.
October: Eighteen U.S. troops are killed in Somalia; Bin Laden later claims that Arab Afghans were involved in the ambush.

1994

March: The United States withdraws its remaining forces from Somalia; Bin Laden eventually gloats that the United States proved itself a "paper tiger" by its retreat.

April: The Saudi government revokes Bin Laden's citizenship.

November: Fearing failure, al Qaeda aborts an assassination plot against U.S. president Bill Clinton in the Philippines.

1995

January: Authorities discover and thwart al Qaeda plots to destroy eleven airliners and assassinate Pope John Paul II.

June: Al Qaeda members fail to assassinate Egyptian president Hosni Mubarak.

November 13: Bin Laden influences an attack on the Saudi-Arabian National Guard Building in Riyadh, killing five Americans and two others.

1996

Spring: Clinton signs a top secret order authorizing the CIA to destroy al Qaeda.

May: Bin Laden leaves Sudan; he returns to Afghanistan, where he begins helping the fundamentalist Taliban movement take control of the country.

June 25: A truck bomb rips through the Khobar military housing complex in Dhahran, Saudi Arabia, killing nineteen U.S. soldiers and one Saudi; Bin Laden and al Qaeda are eventually linked to the attack.

August: Bin Laden issues his first major fatwa, "Declaration of War Against the Americans Occupying the Land of the Two Holy Places."

1997

May: Pakistan and Saudi Arabia recognize the Taliban as the government of Afghanistan.

November 17: Bin Laden is suspected of funding the slaughter of sixty-two tourists in Luxor, Egypt; his colleague al-Zawahiri is eventually convicted in absentia by the Egyptian government for the massacre and is sentenced to death.

1998

February: Bin Laden helps found the World Islamic Front for Fighting Jews and Christians; he and other World Islamic Front leaders issue a new fatwa, "Jihad Against Jews and Crusaders."

August 7: Al Qaeda stages two nearly simultaneous bombings of U.S. embassies in Tanzania and Kenya, killing 225 people and wounding more than 4,000 others; this leads to a U.S. attempt to freeze Bin Laden's financial assets.

August 20: Clinton retaliates for the embassy bombings with ineffective missile strikes against Sudan and Afghanistan.

November: The Manhattan Federal District Court indicts six al Qaeda members for the African embassy attacks, including Bin Laden and the organization's military leader, Mohammed Atef.

1999

Bin Laden's family publicly disowns him.

December: Al Qaeda member Ahmed Ressam is caught trying to cross the Canadian border into the United States with a carload of explosives; he soon admits to planning an attack on the Los Angeles International Airport during the upcoming New Year celebrations; other "millennium attacks" planned by al Qaeda against the United States and Israel are thwarted by authorities.

2000

October 12: The destroyer USS *Cole* in the port of Aden is attacked by suicide bombers; the attack was personally planned by Bin Laden; seventeen sailors are killed and thirty-nine others injured.

2001

January: Counterterrorism chief Richard Clarke issues a memo to National Security Adviser Condoleezza Rice warning of al Qaeda's threat to America; no action is taken on the memo until September 4.

May: A U.S. court finds four al Qaeda members guilty of terrorist acts that include the 1998 U.S. embassy bombings; two of the men are sentenced to death.

September 11: Al Qaeda guerrillas hijack four American airliners; two of the planes are deliberately crashed into the Twin Towers of New York's World Trade Center, another into the Pentagon; the fourth airliner crashes near Shanksville, Pennsylvania; overall, nearly three thousand people are killed.

September 15: President George W. Bush announces that the United States is at war against Bin Laden and al Qaeda.

October: U.S.-led forces invade Afghanistan.

November: Al Qaeda's military commander Atef is killed in Afghanistan.

December: The Taliban government collapses; Bin Laden escapes capture or death during the Battle of Tora Bora; a videotape surfaces in which he appears to discuss his prior knowledge of the 9/11 attacks with several followers; al Qaeda member Zacarias Moussaoui (previously arrested on an immigration violation) is charged with involvement in the 9/11 attacks.

2002

Al Qaeda is linked to several attacks, including an April 11 bombing of a synagogue in Tunisia and two October 12 bomb attacks on nightclubs in the Indonesian island of Bali.

2003

March 20: The United States invades Iraq, based primarily on the belief that Hussein possesses and is ready to use weapons of mass destruction (WMDs); Bush considers this invasion part of America's war on terror, which is also directed at al Qaeda and Bin Laden.
April 9: The Iraqi capital of Baghdad falls to U.S.-led forces.
May 1: Bush announces an end to major combat operations in Iraq.
December 13: Hussein is captured by U.S. forces.

2004

March 11: A series of commuter train explosions in Madrid, Spain, kill nearly two hundred people and wound more than eighteen hundred. Basque separatists are initially blamed for the bombing, but it soon becomes evident that Islamic extremists, possibly with al Qaeda connections, are responsible.
March 14: Spanish voters oust leaders who have supported the United States in Iraq.
March 18: The U.S. House of Representatives unanimously votes to raise the reward for Bin Laden's capture from $25 million to $50 million.
April: Bin Laden offers a truce to European nations who abandon their support for the U.S. occupation of Iraq.
September 8: The number of Americans killed in Iraq passes one thousand; most casualties have taken place during the guerrilla insurgency that followed the fall of Hussein's government in May 2003.
September 30: In a presidential election debate against Bush, Democratic candidate John Kerry argues that U.S. involvement in Iraq has hampered the war against Bin Laden and al Qaeda.
October: Bin Laden issues a videotaped message to the American people, promising further attacks unless the United States changes its Middle East policies; for the first time, he acknowledges his involvement in the 9/11 attacks; John Lehman, 9/11 Commission member, announces that Bin Laden is hiding in South Waziristan, a region of Pakistan, but cannot currently be captured or killed.
November: Bush is reelected, largely because of public confidence in his national security policies.

December: Bin Laden issues an audiotaped message praising the Iraqi insurgency led by Jordanian-born Abu Musab al-Zarqawi; Bin Laden also urges Iraqis to boycott their upcoming democratic election.

2005

January: Defying insurgency attacks and Bin Laden's taped message, Iraqis hold a successful election. The White House admits to having found no evidence of weapons of mass destruction (WMDs) in Iraq.

March 1: U.S. intelligence authorities reveal that they have intercepted a communication between Bin Laden and Iraqi insurgency leader al-Zarqawi; analysts believe the conversation hints at further attacks against the United States.

March 12: The Islamic Commission of Spain marks the anniversary of the 2004 Madrid bombings by issuing the first legitimate fatwa against Bin Laden and al Qaeda, condemning them as outside the Islamic faith and denouncing all acts of terrorism.

GLOSSARY

Note: spellings of Arabic words and names will vary depending on their source.

Afghan Arabs (Arab Afghans): Non-Afghans who fought against the Soviets during the war in Afghanistan (1979–1989). Though named "Arabs," some of these foreign fighters were not Arabian.

AK-47: A Soviet-designed automatic rifle.

apparatchik: An official who is blindly devoted to an organization, cause, or leader (a Russian term).

bayat: An oath of allegiance.

burka: An all-covering garment worn by many Muslim women.

caliph: The religious and political leader of the **caliphate**; a successor to the prophet Muhammad.

caliphate: A theocracy encompassing the Islamic world, ruled by a **caliph**.

din: Obedience and submission to God; a mode of personal conduct based on religion.

emir: An Islamic ruler, chief, or commander.

fard 'ayn: An action which is required of every Muslim.

fard kifayah: An action which is required of the Muslim community, but not necessarily of every individual Muslim.

fatwa: A religious and legal opinion or decree (seldom a declaration of war or hostile intent).

fiqh: Islamic jurisprudence; an understanding of Islamic law.

ghaybah: Absence or concealment; a state of being divinely withdrawn from men or being made invisible by God.

hadith: Written records of the sayings and deeds of the prophet Muhammad; reports on the **sunna**.

hajj: Pilgrimage to the holy city of Mecca.

haram: A prohibited act or deed.

Hejaz: A region of Arabia that includes the cities of Mecca, Medina, Jeddah, and at-Ta'if.

hijab: The covering of Muslim women with veils or other clothing.

imam: A high-ranking religious leader.

iman: Faith and trust in Allah.

jahiliyya: Ignorance, disregard, or rejection of Islam.

Al Jazeera: An Arabic television news network based in the nation of Qatar.

jihad: Struggle or striving.

kaffir: (plural: kuffar) A denier or unbeliever; typically applied to a non-Muslim.

madrassa: Islamic school.

Mahdi: A divinely guided Islamic leader; an Islamic messiah.

mahram: A man whom a woman may not marry because of marital or blood kinship.

mosque: An Islamic place of worship.

mujahid: (plural: mujahideen) An Islamic holy warrior.

qiblah: The direction of Mecca, which every Muslim must face in prayer five times daily.

rial: The currency of Qatar and Saudi Arabia.

al-Saud: The ruling royal family of Saudi Arabia.

shaheed: (plural: shuhadaa) Witness or martyr.

sharia: Traditional Islamic law.

sheikh: A respected elder; a wise person.

Shia: The second-largest sect of Islam.

shura: Consultation, usually of a community by its ruler (**emir**).

Stinger missile: A handheld antiaircraft weapon.

Sufi: A mystical form of Islam.

sunna: The sayings and deeds of the prophet Muhammad, as recorded in the **hadith**.

Sunni: The largest sect of Islam.

tatarrus: The use of civilians as "human shields" in battle.

ulema: The community of Islamic legal scholars.

umma: The Islamic community as a whole.

FOR FURTHER RESEARCH

STATEMENTS AND WRITINGS BY OSAMA BIN LADEN

Tayseer Alouni, "Transcript of Bin Laden's October Interview," *CNN.com*, February 2, 2002. http://archives.cnn. transcript/index.html. In an October 2001 interview with an Al Jazeera correspondent, Osama bin Laden praises the attacks of 9/11 without acknowledging direct involvement in them.

Peter Arnett, "CNN March 1997 Interview with Osama bin Laden," *FindLaw.com*. http://news.findlaw.com. In an interview with CNN reporter Peter Arnett, Bin Laden discusses his declaration of jihad against the United States and remembers the Soviet-Afghan War.

Osama bin Laden, "Bin Laden Tape: Text," *BBC News*, February 12, 2003. http://news.bbc.co.uk. A purported Bin Laden audio message broadcast on Arabic television condemns the U.S. war in Iraq and encourages Iraqis to fight their invaders.

——, "Full Text: Bin Laden's 'Letter to America,'" *Observer*, November 24, 2002. http://observer.guardian.co.uk. A purported Bin Laden message circulated via the Internet warns of further attacks against the West and describes Muslims as "eager for martyrdom."

——, "Full Text: 'Bin Laden's Message,'" *BBC News*, November 12, 2002. http://news.bbc.co.uk. In a message broadcast by Arabic television, Bin Laden describes members of the U.S. administration as "gangsters" and "the biggest butchers of this age."

——, "Full Text: 'Bin Laden' Tape," *BBC News*, January 4, 2004. http://news.bbc.co.uk. An audiotape message purportedly by Bin Laden describes the U.S. occupation of Iraq as "a link in the Zionist-crusader chain of evil."

——, "Full Transcript of Bin Laden's Speech," *Aljazeera.net*,

November 1, 2004. http://english.aljazeera.net. In a videotaped message to the American people prior to the 2004 presidential election, Bin Laden finally acknowledges his complicity in the attacks of September 11, 2001.

——, "Jihad Against Jews and Crusaders," *Washingtonpost. com.* www.washingtonpost.com. On February 23, 1998, Bin Laden and other Islamic militants issued a second fatwa (religious decree), announcing that killing Western soldiers and civilians alike is "an individual duty" for Muslims everywhere.

——, "Ladenese Epistle: Declaration of War," *Washingtonpo st.com*, 2001. www.washingtonpost.com. On August 23, 1996, Bin Laden issued his first fatwa, condemning the Saudi regime for its relations with the West and promising glory to martyred Islamic warriors.

——, "Message to Iraqis," *Aljazeera.net*, October 19, 2003. http://english.aljazeera.net. In a speech broadcast on Arabic television, Bin Laden encourages Iraqi insurgents and calls democracy "the faith of the ignorant."

——, "Message to U.S." *Aljazeera.net*, October 18, 2003. http://english.aljazeera.net. In a speech broadcast on Arabic television, Bin Laden denounces the American people for numerous crimes against humanity, including the occupation of Iraq.

——, "Mujahid Usamah Bin Ladin Talks Exclusively to *Nida'ul Islam* About the New Powder Keg in the Middle East," *Nida'ul Islam*, October/November 1996. www. islam.org. In an interview with an Australian Islamist publication, Bin Laden calls upon Muslims everywhere to oppose the West.

——, "Osama Claims He Has Nukes," *Dawn.com*, November 10, 2001. www.dawn.com. In an interview with the Pakistani newspaper *Dawn*, Bin Laden claims that al Qaeda possesses weapons of mass destruction "as a deterrent" against America.

——, "Special Dispatch Series—No. 476," Middle East Media Research Institute, March 5, 2003. www.memri.org/bin/ articles.cgi?Page=subjects&Area=jihad&ID=SP47603. In a sermon delivered on 'Id al-Adha (the Feast of Sacrifice), Bin Laden warns Muslims that the West intends to destroy the Islamic world.

——, "Special Dispatch Series—No. 539," Middle East Media Research Institute, July 18, 2003. www.memri.org/bin/

articles.cgi?Page=subjects&Area=jihad&ID=SP53903. In a speech posted on the Internet, Bin Laden discusses the meaning and nature of jihad.

——, "Special Dispatch Series—No. 695," Middle East Media Research Institute, April 15, 2004. www.memri.org/bin/articles.cgi?Page=archives&Area=sd&ID=SP69504. In a speech broadcast on Arabic television, Bin Laden offers peace to European nations that refuse to support the U.S-led occupation of Iraq.

——, "Transcript of Usama Bin Laden Video Tape," U.S. Department of Defense, December 13, 2001. www.defenselink.mil/news/Dec2001/d20011213ubl.pdf. In a tape released by the U.S. government, Bin Laden tells several followers that he had advance knowledge of the attacks of September 11, 2001.

——, "Usamah Bin-Ladin, the Destruction of the Base," Terrorism Research Center, June 10, 1999. http://web.archive.org. In an interview broadcast by Al Jazeera on June 10, 1999, Bin Laden reflects upon the Soviet defeat in Afghanistan and anticipates the fall of the United States as a superpower.

John Miller, "Interview Osama bin Laden," *Frontline*, May 1998. www.pbs.org. In a May 1998 interview, Osama bin Laden talks about his political goals and his life as the world's most wanted criminal.

Rahimullah Yusufzai, "Exclusive Interview: 'Conversation with Terror,'" *Time*, January 11, 1999. www.time.com. Osama bin Laden praises terrorist attacks against the West and says that acquiring weapons of mass destruction is "a religious duty" for Islamic militants.

Writings on Osama bin Laden and al Qaeda

Yonah Alexander and Michael S. Swetnam, *Usama bin Laden's al-Qaida: Profile of a Terrorist Network*. Ardsley, NY: Transnational, 2001.

Anonymous [Michael Scheuer], *Through Our Enemies' Eyes: Osama bin Laden, Radical Islam, and the Future of America*. Washington, DC: Brassey's, 2003.

Peter L. Bergen, *Holy War, Inc.: Inside the Secret World of Osama bin Laden*. New York: Touchstone, 2002.

Yossef Bodansky, *Bin Laden: The Man Who Declared War on America*. Roseville, CA: Prima, 1999.

Jason Burke, *Al-Qaeda: Casting a Shadow of Terror.* New York: I.B. Tauris, 2004.

——, "The Making of the World's Most Wanted Man," *Observer,* October 28, 2001.

Jane Corbin, *Al-Qaeda: In Search of the Terror Network That Threatens the World.* New York: Nation, 2002.

Mantoshe Singh Devji, *The Mad Messiah: Osama bin Laden and the Seeds of Terror.* Scottsdale, AZ: Inkwell, 2002.

Christopher Hitchens, "Blaming bin Laden First," *Nation,* October 22, 2001.

Roland Jacquard, *In the Name of Osama Bin Laden: Global Terrorism and the Bin Laden Brotherhood.* Trans. George Holoch. Durham, NC: Duke University Press, 2002.

Samuel M. Katz, *Relentless Pursuit: The DSS and the Manhunt for the Al-Qaeda Terrorists.* New York: Forge, 2002.

Bill Loehfelm, *Osama bin Laden.* Farmington Hills, MI: Lucent, 2003.

John Miller, "A Conversation with the Most Dangerous Man in the World," *Esquire,* February 1, 1999.

Simon Reeve, *The New Jackals: Ramzi Yousef, Osama bin Laden and the Future of Terrorism.* Boston: Northeastern University Press, 1999.

Adam Robinson, *Bin Laden: Behind the Mask of the Terrorist.* New York: Arcade 2002.

Mary Anne Weaver, "The Real bin Laden," *New Yorker,* January 24, 2000.

WRITINGS ON THE WAR ON TERROR

J.L. Anderson and Thomas Dworzak, *Taliban.* London: Trolley, 2003.

Anonymous, *Imperial Hubris: Why the West Is Losing the War on Terror.* Washington, DC: Brassey's, 2004.

Robert Baer, *See No Evil: The True Story of a Ground Soldier in the CIA's War on Terrorism.* New York: Three Rivers, 2003.

Mark Bowden, *Black Hawk Down: A Story of Modern War.* New York: Atlantic Monthly Press, 1999.

Matthew Brzezinski, *Fortress America: On the Front Lines of*

Homeland Security—An Inside Look at the Coming Surveillance State. New York: Bantam, 2004.

Noam Chomsky, *9-11.* New York: Seven Stories, 2001.

Richard A. Clarke, *Against All Enemies: Inside America's War on Terror.* New York: Free Press, 2004.

Stephen Flynn, *America the Vulnerable: How Our Government Is Failing to Protect Us from Terrorism.* New York: Perennial, 2005.

Bill Gertz, *Breakdown: How America's Intelligence Failures Led to September 11.* Washington, DC: Regnery, 2002.

Richard Labévière, *Dollars for Terror: The United States and Islam.* Trans. Martin Demers. New York: Algora, 2000.

National Commission on Terrorist Attacks, *The 9/11 Commission Report: Final Report of the National Commission on Terrorist Attacks upon the United States.* New York: W.W. Norton, 2004.

Benjamin Orbach, "Usama bin Laden and Al-Qa'ida: Origins and Doctrines," *Middle East Review of International Affairs (MERIA) Journal.* December 2001.

Norman Podhoretz, "World War IV: How It Started, What It Means, and Why We Have to Win," *Commentary,* February 2002.

Ahmed Rashid, *Jihad: The Rise of Militant Islam in Central Asia.* New Haven, CT: Yale University Press, 2002.

——, *Taliban: Militant Islam, Oil and Fundamentalism in Central Asia.* New Haven, CT: Yale University Press, 2001.

WRITINGS ON ISLAM AND RADICAL ISLAMISM

M.A. Ashraf, "True Islamic Teachings Compared to Al-Qaeda's Doctrine," *Review of Religions,* April 2004.

Raymond William Baker, *Islam Without Fear: Egypt and the New Islamists.* Cambridge, MA: Harvard University Press, 2003.

Larry Diamond, Marc F. Plattner, and Daniel Brumberg, eds., *Islam and Democracy in the Middle East.* Baltimore: Johns Hopkins University Press, 2003.

Carl W. Ernst, *Following Muhammad: Rethinking Islam in the Contemporary World.* Chapel Hill: University of North Carolina Press, 2003.

Yohanan Friedmann, *Tolerance and Coercion in Islam: Interfaith Relations in the Muslim Tradition.* Cambridge: Cambridge University Press, 2003.

Graham E. Fuller, *The Future of Political Islam.* New York: Palgrave Macmillan, 2004.

Samuel P. Huntington, *The Clash of Civilizations and the Remaking of World Order.* New York: Touchstone, 1997.

Abdelwahab Meddeb, *The Malady of Islam.* Trans. Pierre Joris and Ann Reid. New York: Basic Books, 2003.

Sayyid Qutb, *Milestones.* Rev. ed. Indianapolis: American Trust, 1991.

B.A. Robertson, ed., *Shaping the Current Islamic Reformation.* London: Frank Cass, 2003.

Omid Safi, ed., *Progressive Muslims on Justice, Gender, and Pluralism.* Oxford: Oneworld, 2003.

Ibn Warraq, ed., *Leaving Islam: Apostates Speak Out.* Amherst, NY: Prometheus, 2003.

WEB SITES

Aljazeera.net, http://english.aljazeera.net. *Al Jazeera* is an Arabic television network based in the small nation of Qatar. Its English-language Web site offers information and insights into Bin Laden, al Qaeda, radical Islam, and current events in the Islamic world that are sometimes difficult to find in the Western media. Though sometimes criticized by the U.S. government as biased, *Al Jazeera* has a reputation throughout most of the rest of the world for journalistic balance and excellence.

The National Security Archive, www.gwu.edu. The U.S. Freedom of Information Act went into effect in 1967, placing limits on secrecy within the federal government. The privately funded National Security Archive uses the Freedom of Information Act to post recently unclassified documents on its Web site. Recently, many of these have pertained to Osama bin Laden, al Qaeda, and the war on terror.

Terrorism Research Center, Inc. (TRC), www.terrorism.com. The TRC is an independent institute dedicated to studying political violence. Its Web site offers valuable scholarship, commentary, and documents, and is often used as an information source by the *The New York Times,*

Newsweek, National Public Radio, CNN, and many other media news outlets.

Understanding-Islam.org, www.understanding-islam.com. This Web site, affiliated with the Al-Mawrid Institute of Islamic Sciences, offers useful information about the religion of Islam; it also includes discussions among mainstream Muslims about issues and controversies of contemporary Islam, including the nature of jihad and the rights of women.

The United States government maintains several Web sites rich in both secondary sources (including press releases and news stories) and primary sources (including speeches by political leaders). Material on Osama bin Laden and the war on terror can be found at these three government Web sites:

The U.S. Defense Department, www.defenselink.mil.

The U.S. State Department, http://usinfo.state.gov.

The White House, www.whitehouse.gov.

INDEX

May 20 2011 — We got'em. Merica!!
USA! USA! USA USA! USA!